"It is good to have Lanier and Ross as rel
ing domain of the Greek Old Testamer
achievement: introducing the complexi
simple way without compromising accu
    Peter J. Williams, Principal, Tynda_ _._.u.u.., Cambridge

"Pastors and seminary students regularly ask me about the Septuagint and its
significance for a modern, English-speaking Christian. *The Septuagint: What
It Is and Why It Matters* is my new number-one recommended resource for
these inquiries. The book is informed by a scholarly knowledge of the subject,
yet it remains accessible and a pleasure to read."
    Robert L. Plummer, Collin and Evelyn Aikman Professor of Biblical
    Studies, The Southern Baptist Theological Seminary; Founder and
    Host, Daily Dose of Greek

"Interested in the Septuagint? Start here. This accessible introduction carefully navigates the *what* and the *so what* of the Septuagint, charting a steady
course through a quagmire of complex issues. Tricky matters are treated with
scholarly precision and theological sensitivity, and readers will find a correc-
tive both to an overemphasis and to an underemphasis on the Septuagint.
This book will be useful to the beginning student, the graduate student, the
pastor, and anyone interested in learning more about how we got the Bible."
    Brandon D. Crowe, Professor of New Testament, Westminster
    Theological Seminary

"In class I'm regularly asked how much value and authority we should attribute to the Septuagint. The answer is complex, but students are looking
for clear answers. As a teacher, I had yet to come across a clear yet precise
resource explaining the origins and role of the Septuagint—until now. Lanier
and Ross have produced a book I will be recommending each time this question is posed. I highly recommend it."
    Patrick Schreiner, Associate Professor of New Testament and Biblical
    Theology, Midwestern Baptist Theological Seminary

"The Septuagint is unfamiliar and intimidating to most Bible students. I don't know of a more accessible introduction than this book."

Andrew David Naselli, Associate Professor of Systematic Theology and New Testament, Bethlehem College & Seminary; Pastor, Bethlehem Baptist Church

"The Septuagint is a minefield of quandaries for both Bible scholar and devoted layperson: Why is the Septuagint in my Bible's footnotes, offering a different reading from the main text or the source for the reading in the main text? Why do the New Testament authors quote from the Septuagint and not the Hebrew? In this book, Lanier and Ross know the minefield and ably guide readers through the potential dangers related to terminology, the task of ancient translation, textual and translational histories, canonical formation, and biblical authority and lead them safely to the other side. I happily recommend this book!"

John D. Meade, Associate Professor of Old Testament; Codirector, Text & Canon Institute, Phoenix Seminary; coauthor, *The Biblical Canon Lists from Early Christianity*

The Septuagint

The Septuagint

What It Is and Why It Matters

Gregory R. Lanier and William A. Ross

WHEATON, ILLINOIS

Library of Congress Cataloging-in-Publication Data

Names: Lanier, Gregory R., author. | Ross, William A., 1987– author.
Title: The Septuagint : what it is and why it matters / Gregory R. Lanier and William A. Ross.
Description: Wheaton : Crossway, 2021. | Includes bibliographical references and index.
Identifiers: LCCN 2020049309 (print) | LCCN 2020049310 (ebook) | ISBN 9781433570520 (trade paperback) | ISBN 9781433570537 (pdf) | ISBN 9781433570544 (mobi) | ISBN 9781433570551 (epub)
Subjects: LCSH: Bible. Old Testament Greek—Versions—Septuagint—Introductions.
Classification: LCC BS744 .L36 2021 (print) | LCC BS744 (ebook) | DDC 221.4/8—dc23
LC record available at https://lccn.loc.gov/2020049309
LC ebook record available at https://lccn.loc.gov/2020049310

---

*To the students who bravely take our Septuagint electives
and humor their professors' excessive zeal about obscure topics.
You're secretly our favorites.*

Contents

Tables

Abbreviations

ABBREVIATIONS OF ANCIENT WORKS (e.g., *Ag. Ap.* for *Against Apion*, by Josephus) follow §8 of *The SBL Handbook of Style*, 2nd ed. (Atlanta: SBL, 2014).

ABS	Archaeology and Biblical Studies
Ag. Ap.	*Against Apion*, by Josephus
Ant.	*Jewish Antiquities*, by Josephus
Anton.	*Antonius*, by Plutarch
ASNU	Acta Seminarii Neotestamentici Upsaliensis
BASOR	*Bulletin of the American Schools of Oriental Research*
B. Bat.	*Baba Batra* (Talmud text)
BBR	*Bulletin of Biblical Research*
BCAW	Blackwell Companions to the Ancient World
BETL	Bibliotheca Ephemeridum Theologicarum Lovaniensium
Bib	*Biblica*
BIOSCS	*Bulletin of the International Organization of Septuagint and Cognate Studies*
BJS	Brown Judaic Studies

BPT	*Biblica et Patristica Thoruniensia*
BTS	Biblical Tools and Studies
CBET	Contributions to Biblical Exegesis and Theology
Civ.	*De civitate Dei*, by Augustine
Comm. Isa.	*Commentariorum in Isaiam libri XVIII*, by Jerome
Comm. Jo.	*Commentarii in evangelium Joannis*, by Origen
Comm. Matt.	*Commentarium in evangelium Matthaei*, by Origen
Comm. Tit.	*Commentariorum in epistulam ad Titum liber*, by Jerome
ConBOT	Coniectanea Biblica: Old Testament Series
Contempl.	*De vita contemplativa*, by Philo
CRINT	Compendia Rerum Iudaicarum ad Novum Testamentum
CrSHB	Critical Studies in the Hebrew Bible
CTL	Cambridge Textbooks in Linguistics
De mens.	*De mensuribus et ponderibus*, by Epiphanius
Dial.	*Dialogus cum Tryphone*, by Justin Martyr
Doctr. chr.	*De doctrina christiana*, by Augustine
Ep. Afr.	*Epistula ad Africanum*, by Origen
ESV mg.	ESV marginal note
ET	English translation
1 Apol.	*First Apology*, by Justin Martyr
Flacc.	*In Flaccum*, by Philo
Geogr.	*Geographica*, by Strabo
Haer.	*Adversus haereses*, by Irenaeus
Hist.	*Eusebii historia ecclesiastica a Rufino translata et continuata*, by Rufinus
Hist. eccl.	*Historia ecclesiastica*, by Eusebius

JAJ	*Journal of Ancient Judaism*
JETS	*Journal of the Evangelical Theological Society*
JNSL	*Journal of Northwest Semitic Languages*
JSJ	*Journal for the Study of Judaism*
JSJSup	Supplements to the Journal for the Study of Judaism
JSNTSup	Journal for the Study of the New Testament Supplement Series
JSOTSup	Journal for the Study of the Old Testament Supplement Series
JTS	*Journal of Theological Studies*
Jub.	Jubilees
LCC	Library of Christian Classics
LCL	Loeb Classical Library
Leg.	*Legum allegoriae*, by Philo
Legat.	*Legatio ad Gaium*, by Philo
LES	Lexham English Septuagint
Let. Aris.	Letter of Aristeas
LHBOTS	Library of Hebrew Bible / Old Testament Studies
LXX	An abbreviation commonly used for the Septuagint, variously defined
LXX.H	Handbuch zur Septuaginta
Mos.	*De vita Mosis*, by Philo
MT	Masoretic Text
NETS	New English Translation of the Septuagint
NovT	*Novum Testamentum*
NovTSup	Supplements to Novum Testamentum
NT	New Testament
OBO	Orbis Biblicus et Orientalis

OG	Old Greek
OLA	Orientalia Lovaniensia Analecta
OT	Old Testament
OTS	Old Testament Studies
OtSt	Oudtestamentische Studiën
P.Oxy.	Oxyrhynchus Papyrus
Praef. ad Par.	*Praefatio in libro Paralipomenon*, by Jerome
Praef. ad Sal.	*Praefatio in libros Salomonis*, by Jerome
Praep. Ev.	*Praeparatio evangelica*, by Eusebius
Pr. Azar.	Prayer of Azariah
P.Ryl.	Rylands Papyrus
r.	reigned
Rahlfs-Hanhart	Rahlfs, Alfred, and Robert Hanhart, eds. *Septuaginta: Editio altera*. Stuttgart: Deutsche Bibelgesellschaft, 2006.
RB	*Revue biblique*
RESt	*Review of Ecumenical Studies*
SCS	Septuagint and Cognate Studies
SEC	*Semitica et Classica*
SJOT	*Scandinavian Journal of the Old Testament*
SNTSMS	Society for New Testament Studies Monograph Series
Somn.	*De somniis*, by Philo
STDJ	Studies on the Texts of the Desert of Judah
Strom.	*Stromateis*, by Clement of Alexandria
TBN	*Themes in Biblical Narrative*
TENTS	Texts and Editions for New Testament Study
Text	*Textus*
Them	*Themelios*

TSAJ	Texte und Studien zum antiken Judentum
UBW	Understanding the Bible and Its World
VCSup	Supplements to Vigiliae Christianae
Vit. Const.	*Vita Constantini*, by Eusebius
VTSup	Supplements to Vetus Testamentum
WTJ	*Westminster Theological Journal*
WUNT	Wissenschaftliche Untersuchungen zum Neuen Testament
ZAW	*Zeitschrift für die alttestamentliche Wissenschaft*
ZNW	*Zeitschrift für die neutestamentliche Wissenschaft*

Introduction

NOT MANY PEOPLE KNOW MUCH about the Septuagint. This is just as true of the majority of churchgoing Christians as it is of many religion students and even pastors. Nor is it all that surprising.

Many pastors find it challenging enough to get their people to read the Old Testament in English, let alone become familiar with its ancient Greek translation. Devout Bible readers rarely stop to consult the cryptic marginal notes that mention the Septuagint, even though it appears as early as Genesis 2:2 in the CSB and Genesis 4:8 in the ESV and NIV.

With pressures hitting higher education from all sides, the typical religion curriculum barely has enough room already for courses on church history, theology, and Bible introduction. Should ministers-in-training really spend time learning the intricate textual history of the Bible rather than, say, counseling or preaching? After all, how often can the Septuagint possibly be relevant in sermon preparation? These pragmatic reasons and others like them have led many to conclude that this area of study is excusably ignored.

Yet this book exists, and you are reading it—two facts that attest to growing interest in the Septuagint. This growth is mostly concentrated among scholars and zealous students. But like some scholarly trends, it is beginning to get attention outside those circles as well. There are several reasons for this wider interest: questions about the text of the Old Testament and its reliability, lack of clarity about the formation of the Old Testament canon, and affirmations—or denials—of the importance of the Septuagint for New Testament authors. Each issue merits serious reflection by thoughtful Bible readers.

To this end, a few introductions to the Septuagint have appeared in recent years.[1] Why write another? This book aims to accomplish what even we as the authors occasionally thought was an impossible task: to distill the enormous complexity surrounding the origins, transmission, and role of the Septuagint into a brief introduction that is accessible to laypeople but still informative for scholars. Achieving this goal requires delving into some details that may be novel and complex for newcomers (press on!), while avoiding other details that may be expected by specialists (forgive us!). A true "introduction" that is around 200 pages and does not require knowledge of the biblical languages cannot say everything that could be said.[2] So we focus on answering two big questions, broken down into smaller subtopics.

In part 1, we answer the question "What is the Septuagint?" by covering the following topics:

Chap. 1: The basics of the "Septuagint" and why that label is somewhat problematic

Chap. 2: The origins of the translation (who and where from)

---

1 Especially Karen H. Jobes and Moisés Silva, *Invitation to the Septuagint*, 2nd ed. (Grand Rapids, MI: Baker Academic, 2015).

2 For comparison, the volume by Jobes and Silva is over 400 pages, often assuming experience in Greek and Hebrew.

Chap. 3: The approach(es) used in translating the Hebrew Bible into Greek

Chap. 4: The transmission of the Greek texts throughout history

Part 1 gives readers a broad working knowledge about the Septuagint. In part 2, we address the question "Why does it matter?" by covering the following topics:

Chap. 5: The value of the Septuagint for studying the Old Testament (canon, text, and interpretation)

Chap. 6: The value of the Septuagint for studying the New Testament (adoption by the early church, influence on New Testament style/ vocabulary, and use in Old Testament quotations)

Chap. 7: The nature of the Septuagint's authority for today's church

Part 2 introduces readers to the many ways in which a working knowledge of the Septuagint is vital for Christians today.

The book concludes with a snapshot of the ten things a minister or Bible teacher should know (and teach) about the Septuagint, including a selected bibliography of key resources for further study.

PART 1

WHAT IS THE SEPTUAGINT?

What (If Anything) Is the So-Called Septuagint?

ON THE SURFACE, "SEPTUAGINT" is a term applied to the collection of Israel's Scriptures in Greek. But there are many complexities under the surface of that deceptively simple definition. Before delving into them in the chapters that follow, we first need to explain more clearly what exactly the so-called Septuagint is and is not—and whether that term is even useful. We will seek to do this by addressing two issues:

1. The backdrop of the Hebrew Bible: What aspects of the Hebrew Bible do people need to understand before discussing its Greek translation?
2. The challenge of terminology: What are unhelpful ways to conceptualize the Septuagint, and what is the best way to label this collection of Greek texts?

Discussing these topics here lays a foundation for answering the questions posed in subsequent chapters.

The Backdrop of the Hebrew Bible

To speak about the Septuagint is to presume the Hebrew Bible.[1] In some ways, that presumption is obvious, since one is essentially a translation of the other. But there are less obvious (or less understood) aspects of the Hebrew Bible that are critical for avoiding Septuagint pitfalls right out of the gate.

The Old Testament Today

Virtually all modern editions of the Old Testament on the market today are translations of the ancient Hebrew Bible. As stated in their introductory pages, these translations are based on a particular tradition known as the Masoretic Text (MT).[2] The best complete manuscript of the Masoretic Text is the Leningrad Codex, which dates to the early eleventh century AD, though it reliably preserves a written tradition that is much older.

At the same time, modern Old Testament translations also include footnotes that refer to wording found in ancient texts that does not match the Masoretic Text that they are otherwise translating. For instance, the ESV footnote at Genesis 4:8 says, "Samaritan, Septuagint, Syriac, Vulgate add *Let us go out to the field*." Or at Genesis 4:15, the NIV main text reads, "Not so," but the footnote says, "Septuagint, Vulgate and Syriac; Hebrew *Very well*." The majority of these differences are minor. But some are significant, which we will consider later.

---

1 In scholarly circles, some prefer to avoid the term Old Testament since it presumes a Christian perspective. Since that is our perspective, we use that term without reservation. We also use the term Hebrew Bible, however, when precision about the ancient language and texts is needed.

2 The standard scholarly edition of the entire Hebrew Bible is Karl Elliger and Wilhelm Rudolph, eds., *Biblia Hebraica Stuttgartensia* (Stuttgart: Deutsche Bibelgesellschaft, 1977).

Such footnotes indicate that the Masoretic Text—while very reliable and ancient overall—is not perfect and does not by itself contain the singular "original" text of the Old Testament.

The point here is to note that the Hebrew text used for modern Bible translations is not absolutely identical to what was circulating thousands of years ago when Scripture was being written—*nor* to what the ancient Greek translators had in front of them. So it is important to get a sense for where the Hebrew Bible came from and how the differences in wording (like those we see in modern Bible footnotes) began to enter the picture.

The Earliest Copies of Scripture in Hebrew

As the Hebrew Scriptures were recorded over the centuries, the text was written and copied by hand (as were all texts prior to the printing press). Most ancient writing was done on stone, clay tablets, wood, parchment, and even metal. Because Scripture was more esteemed as a written text, it was likely written on sheets of papyrus or leather, which were joined into a roll called a *megillah* or *sepher*.[3]

Because of the intricacies of early writing systems (like cuneiform), writing in much of the ancient world was a specialized task. But with the development of simpler alphabetic scripts between 2000 and 1500 BC, literacy among the general population grew.[4] Among

---

3 A kind of reed pen was probably the typical writing tool. Emanuel Tov, *Scribal Practices and Approaches Reflected in the Texts Found in the Judean Desert*, STDJ 54 (Leiden: Brill, 2004), 29–52. For an overview of ancient writing technology, see Christopher A. Rollston, *Writing and Literacy in the World of Ancient Israel: Epigraphic Evidence from the Iron Age*, ABS 11 (Atlanta: SBL, 2010).

4 Rollston, *Writing*, 19–46; William M. Schniedewind, "Writing and Book Production in the Ancient Near East," in *The New Cambridge History of the Bible*, vol. 1, *From the Beginnings to 600*, ed. James Carleton Paget and Joachim Schaper (Cambridge: Cambridge University Press, 2013), 46, 56.

Israelites it appears that some portion of the population could read and perhaps write at a basic level (e.g., Deut. 6:9; Judg. 8:14).[5]

By the time of David a system of professional training had likely emerged for Hebrew scribes in association with the Jerusalem palace and temple (e.g., 2 Sam. 8:16–18; 1 Kings 4:1–6; 2 Kings 18:18).[6] Given the importance of the monarchy and religious practice within Israelite society (e.g., Deut. 17:18–19), scribal training focused on recording and copying written documents with as much consistency and accuracy as possible. Foremost among these documents was the text of Scripture itself, which had to be reproduced precisely when making extra copies or when scrolls wore out.[7] While many details remain unclear, it appears that certain priestly scribes who were connected with Israel's religious administration preserved the authoritative copies of the sacred writings in a temple archive. This practice continued as long as the temple of Solomon was standing.

Textual Diversification and the Septuagint

The fall of Jerusalem in 586 BC had major consequences for the text of the Hebrew Bible. In their conquest, the Babylonians destroyed the temple, as well as the royal infrastructure that supported it. Many priestly scribes and other officials were killed or exiled, along with the royal court and other well-educated figures (2 Kings 24:14–15;

5   See André Lemaire, *Les écoles et la formation de la Bible dans l'ancien Israël*, OBO 39 (Göttingen: Vandenhoeck & Ruprecht, 1981); Christopher A. Rollston, "Scribal Education in Ancient Israel: The Old Hebrew Epigraphic Evidence," *BASOR* 344 (2006): 47–74.

6   David M. Carr, *The Formation of the Hebrew Bible: A New Reconstruction* (Oxford: Oxford University Press, 2011), 355–85; Karel van der Toorn, *Scribal Culture and the Making of the Hebrew Bible* (Cambridge, MA: Harvard University Press, 2007), 82–96.

7   Alan R. Millard, "In Praise of Ancient Scribes," *Bible & Spade* 2 (1982): 143–53.

Jer. 24:1). Any copies of Scripture that survived the destruction were geographically scattered along with the people.

As the biblical text was copied in disparate areas over the following centuries with much less coordination or oversight by the Jerusalem priesthood, textual variations both large and small inevitably started to enter the picture. Although the reconstruction of the temple around 516 BC reinvigorated priestly scribal activity, some measure of textual diversification of the Hebrew Bible had already begun. The results of this process are visible in the biblical manuscripts of the Dead Sea Scrolls, which were discovered in the 1940s but include scrolls dating as early as the third century BC. Some of these scrolls closely or even perfectly match the much later Masoretic Text tradition. But others differ from the Masoretic Text in nontrivial ways, at both the microlevel (specific words or phrases) and the macrolevel (larger differences in the arrangement or length of books).[8]

These developments do not mean that every copy of Scripture was considered equally valid or equally good in the ancient world. In chapter 7, we discuss the evidence for a standardized temple copy or majority text existing amid other nonstandard texts (such as those found among the Dead Sea Scrolls). But the fact remains: when the Greek translators began their work, a plurality of Hebrew texts was on the scene. Not only did ancient copies of Hebrew Scripture not perfectly match the Hebrew Masoretic Text used for modern translations today, but also ancient copies differed from each other to varying

---

8 Theories abound in explaining this textual diversity. See Ronald S. Hendel, "Assessing the Text-Critical Theories of the Hebrew Bible after Qumran," in *The Oxford Handbook of the Dead Sea Scrolls*, ed. Timothy H. Lim and John J. Collins (Oxford: Oxford University Press, 2012), 281–302. We discuss some of these differences in chap. 5.

degrees. The history of the Hebrew Bible is, ultimately, not as tidy as we might like.

The Challenge of Terminology

The preceding discussion highlights the need to establish concepts and terminology carefully, particularly to avoid pitfalls about what the Septuagint is and is not. Thus far we have been talking somewhat plainly about the "Septuagint," but now we need to refine our terms.

First, as shown above, it is an oversimplification to say that the Septuagint is a Greek translation of *the* Hebrew Bible in a straightforward way, since the translators were not working with a standardized text (or with the same text we use today).

Second, it is an oversimplification to say that the Septuagint is a singular or homogenous entity in itself, as if it were produced in full, at one time, by a single translation committee (like many modern Bible translations). This mistake is common among students, pastors, and even scholars for at least two reasons. First, there is an assumption—often unconscious—that because we can purchase a copy of "the" Septuagint today, it must have come into being in antiquity all at once, like a new publication.[9] But that is not the case, as we discuss in subsequent chapters. Second, the standard terminology itself can perpetuate this misconception: the Septuagint is *called* "the Septuagint." It has a singular title, just like all books, and that can create the impression of coordination and homogeneity.

In the ancient world, however, not only did writing and publishing work differently than it does today, but there is no actual evidence that "the" Septuagint was conceptualized as a singular entity anyhow.

---

9 The standard edition of "the" Septuagint is Alfred Rahlfs and Robert Hanhart, eds., *Septuaginta: Editio altera* (Stuttgart: Deutsche Bibelgesellschaft, 2006).

In fact, we have no evidence for any notion of either unity or uniformity for the Greek translations (note the plural) of the Hebrew Bible as a whole, at any point, anywhere, all the way from the earliest translation efforts to at least the end of the Second Temple period (ca. mid-third century BC through late first century AD).[10] As far as we know, based on ancient writings, including the New Testament, there was no terminology used to refer specifically to Jewish Scriptures written in Greek.

Put differently, Scripture in *Hebrew* and Scripture in *Greek* were apparently not considered qualitatively different in a way that required separate labels. Again, that observation does not rule out certain copies of Scripture (whether Hebrew or Greek) being considered better or worse for various reasons, as discussed in chapter 4. The point here is that numerous texts and versions of the Greek translations of the Hebrew Bible were produced, copied, revised, and circulated among many groups, in many locations, and over several centuries, yet with no uniform title or term to identify those texts as either distinct or unified strictly on the basis of their being written in Greek.

A History of the Term "Septuagint"

So what, if anything, is the "Septuagint"? To put it bluntly, it is a mediocre term of convenience with lots of baggage, but we are probably stuck with it. Yet it did not come out of nowhere. The word "Septuagint" is an English adaptation of the Latin word for the number seventy: *septuaginta*. Likewise, the abbreviation LXX is often used as shorthand for the "Septuagint" because it is the Roman numeral for the number seventy. Why seventy?

---

10 A possible exception might have been the Greek Pentateuch (see chap. 2).

This tradition began with the ancient Greek document known as the Letter of Aristeas, which was written in the Jewish community in Egypt sometime in the second century BC. As discussed in the next chapter, the Letter of Aristeas features a (largely legendary) account of seventy-two Jewish scholars traveling from Jerusalem to Egypt to translate the Pentateuch (Genesis–Deuteronomy) into Greek.

Over the subsequent two millennia, developments occurred in both the grammar and referent of the term *septuaginta* as it was adopted and used in various languages.[11] One development was that the idea of seventy-*two* translators known from the Letter of Aristeas shifted to just seventy (=LXX) translators, possibly as a kind of shorthand.[12] In time, writers began using *septuaginta* ("the seventy") as a way of discussing the Greek translation *as a text*, without mentioning the *translators* themselves.[13] In the medieval and early modern periods, a further shift occurred when writers began to use the number seventy in grammatically *singular* expressions (e.g., *la Septante* in French). As a result, it became much more natural to construe the numerical term (*septuaginta*/LXX) as a title for a singular textual entity, rather than as a reference to the number of translators.[14]

Alongside these grammatical developments, important changes also took place in what was considered part of the "Septuagint" corpus. Originally, in the Letter of Aristeas and other early Jewish writings,

---

11 See Peter J. Williams, "The Bible, the Septuagint, and the Apocrypha: A Consideration of Their Singularity," in *Studies on the Text and Versions of the Hebrew Bible in Honour of Robert Gordon*, ed. Geoffrey Khan and Diana Lipton, VTSup 149 (Leiden: Brill, 2011), 173–78.

12 Josephus, *Ant.* 12.57, 86; Irenaeus, *Haer.* 3.21; Jerome, *Comm. Isa.*, prologue, 18–22.

13 Justin, *Dial.* 120; Augustine, *Civ.* 18.42.

14 Sidney Jellicoe, *The Septuagint and Modern Study* (Oxford: Clarendon, 1968), 57.

only the Greek Pentateuch was in view.[15] But early Christian writers tended to include the translations of other books, if not the entire Old Testament in Greek, under the same term.[16] To make things even more confusing, some early Greek Christian Bibles included certain Apocryphal works. Some of these were Greek translations of books originally written in Hebrew (e.g., Sirach), books originally composed in Greek (e.g., Wisdom of Solomon), or even certain works that were actually Christian in origin (e.g., Odes 12).[17] The practical effect of this history is an imprecise and potentially misleading term: the "Septuagint."

Where Do We Go from Here?

So should we abandon the "Septuagint" as a label? There are two different impulses that lead some to do just that. One is based on a faulty idea of what is actually under discussion, and the other arises from a recognition of the historical and textual complexities discussed above.

The first impulse tends to appear within certain fundamentalist Christian circles that uphold the 1611 King James Version as the only legitimate Bible. At least on the surface, the rationale for this sometimes fiercely held position comes from reverence for the textual basis used for the KJV, often known as the Majority Text (or Textus Receptus). Oftentimes, KJV-only advocates hold the erroneous view that all other Bible versions are textually corrupt and therefore dangerous. Some advocates go to such extremes in this view that they vigorously deny that the "Septuagint" existed at all

---

15 Josephus, *Ant.* 12.48; Philo, *Mos.* 2.25–44.

16 E.g., Justin, *1 Apol.* 31; *Dial.* 71–73; Eusebius, *Hist. eccl.* 6.16.1. See Martin Hengel, *The Septuagint as Christian Scripture: Its Prehistory and the Problem of Its Canon*, OTS (Edinburgh: T&T Clark, 2002); 26–41.

17 See John D. Meade, "Was There a 'Septuagint Canon'?," *Didaktikos* 1, no. 3 (2018): 40–42. We revisit this matter in chaps. 5 and 7.

before the time of Christ, especially because it includes Apocryphal books.[18] The underlying rationale is that because those books are not part of inspired Scripture, it is inconceivable that Jesus and the New Testament authors would have used the "Septuagint" themselves, since doing so would grant legitimacy to the Apocryphal books by extension.[19]

While some aspects of this perspective are understandable, it is fraught with incorrect assumptions. For our purposes, it is enough to point out the faulty ideas about what is actually under discussion when it comes to the "Septuagint." Among those who hold this view, the term is used in a way that implies a stable, unified, and book-like entity with a table of contents that circulated in the ancient world. By now it should be clear that such an understanding is wrong. The textual situation of Scripture in the Second Temple period included nothing of the sort. But it is true that New Testament authors did use the Greek translations of the Hebrew Bible, which raises numerous important questions. We treat that topic in detail in chapter 6 and discuss the implications for the doctrine of Scripture in chapter 7.

The second impulse to dispense with the "Septuagint" as a label is driven by a desire for terminological qualification, nuance, and precision. Often this impulse is characterized by a clear recognition of the very textual complexity in the ancient context that is too often ignored or misunderstood. To be sure, caution is warranted given

---

18 There is, however, undisputed textual evidence for Greek translations of the Hebrew Bible prior to the turn of the era, specifically P.Ryl. 458, which preserves a portion of Deuteronomy and is dated to the second century BC.

19 An excellent discussion of this topic is D. A. Carson, *The King James Version Debate: A Plea for Realism* (Grand Rapids, MI: Baker, 1978).

the laxity and inaccuracies that appear even in the work of seasoned scholars.[20] In most instances, however, scholars do specify how they intend to use their terminology. The most common uses of the following terms are worth summarizing briefly here.[21]

1. Septuagint (LXX)
   a. Used most ambiguously to refer to ancient Jewish Greek Scriptures in general, with no specific text, boundaries, or historical phase in view—which is the sense intended in the title of this book
   b. Used in a slightly more restricted sense to designate the literary boundaries of the corpus, usually as represented in manuscripts like Codex Vaticanus or Codex Alexandrinus and some modern editions, but not necessarily a specific textual form
   c. Used in the historical sense to refer only to the earliest translation of the Greek Pentateuch, as portrayed in the Letter of Aristeas; sometimes also referred to as "the Septuagint proper"
2. Old Greek (OG): A term used to refer to the oldest, original translation of any given book of the Hebrew Bible, in distinction to any later textual revisions or recensions. Scholars tend to regard the best available critical editions of the text in the *Vetus Testamentum Graecum* series (or "the Göttingen edition") as

---

20 See Leonard Greenspoon, "The Use and Abuse of the Term 'LXX' and Related Terminology in Recent Scholarship," *BIOSCS* 20 (1987): 21–29.

21 Karen H. Jobes and Moisés Silva, *Invitation to the Septuagint*, 2nd ed. (Grand Rapids, MI: Baker Academic, 2015), 14–17; Jennifer M. Dines, *The Septuagint*, UBW (London: T&T Clark, 2004), 1–3.

essentially representing the Old Greek, while also understanding that the Old Greek will never be perfectly restored.[22]

3. Septuagint/Old Greek: Sometimes used as a combination of senses 1c and 2, referring to the combined corpus of the original translation of the Greek Pentateuch (LXX) along with the original translations of all other books in the Hebrew Bible (OG)

Even further specificity is possible and sometimes necessary. Yet specificity is not always helpful. For example, only the two *least* specific senses of "Septuagint" (1a and 1b) can include Apocryphal books that were not translated within the purview of what is meant by the "Septuagint."

Concluding Thoughts

For better or worse, there is no universal code of practice among Septuagint scholars. Having discussed the most important aspects of the textual situation for both Hebrew and Greek versions of the Old Testament, we believe it is best to attempt to strike a balance between the two impulses to deny the "Septuagint." In doing so, we hope to avoid fostering conceptual inaccuracy on the one hand and terminological nitpicking on the other. What we need is both an accurate concept of what we are talking about and practical labels for it.

With this in mind, we primarily use the term *Greek Old Testament*, by which we mean the various translations and later revisions of the canonical books of the Hebrew Bible. This term helps avoid the undesirable impression of textual uniformity or stability while also permitting us to use other terms in more specific ways as needed

---

22 For more on the Göttingen edition, see question 2 in the appendix.

(i.e., when discussing noncanonical Jewish Greek writings, including those commonly lumped with the "Septuagint," or various recensions of the Greek Old Testament that differ from what is often labeled the "Septuagint").

The next three chapters add detail to the concepts covered in this chapter, beginning with the important matters of who and where these Greek translations came from.

2

Who and Where Did the Greek Old Testament Come From?

EVERY TRANSLATION OF THE BIBLE is prompted by something, and the Greek Old Testament is no exception. To understand the context and origins of the translation of the Hebrew Bible into Greek, we will proceed in three steps:

1. Egypt in the Hellenistic period: What region and time period is most relevant for understanding the Greek Old Testament as a translation produced by ancient Jews?
2. The (possible) origins of the Greek Pentateuch: What might have caused such a project to get off the ground in the first place?
3. The production of the other Old Testament books in Greek: What do we know about the translation history of the other books in the corpus of Jewish Greek writings?

Addressing such questions familiarizes the reader with a number of important developments in Jewish history prior to the time of Christ that led to the production of the Greek Old Testament. Many of the details remain debated. But scholars agree on the broad contours that should be understood before moving to the Greek translation itself in chapter 3.

Egypt in the Hellenistic Period

Most Bible readers know that the period between the Babylonian exile (586 BC) and the destruction of the Jerusalem temple (AD 70) was extremely tumultuous. Between the composition of the last books of the Old Testament and the earliest books of the New Testament, three major empires successively ruled huge portions of the Mediterranean world.

Of most interest here are the empires of Persia and especially Greece. Beginning in the mid-sixth century, the Persians forged an immense empire under the leadership of Cyrus the Great (r. ca. 559–530 BC). It was the first true world empire and lasted over two centuries. In time, the Persian Empire came to an end thanks to the political and military ingenuity of Philip II of Macedon (r. ca. 359–336 BC) and his son Alexander. After a decisive victory against Darius III at Issus in November 333, Alexander launched an unrelenting campaign that brought numerous territories under his control, establishing the expansive Greek Empire.

Hellenism in Egypt

One of Alexander's conquered territories was Egypt, which offered virtually no resistance. On his arrival in 332, Alexander had himself installed as ruler using the traditional protocol for the enthronement of an Egyptian pharaoh and offered sacrifices to Egyptian gods at Heliopolis and Memphis, the capital. Inaugurating the Greco-Egyptian cultural overlap that would characterize the region for the next several centuries, Alexander then held athletic and musical contests in the traditional Greek fashion. The city he founded in 331—later named Alexandria by Ptolemy I—would become the main cultural and economic center of Egypt for centuries.[1]

When Alexander died on a military campaign in 323, his military power rested with his generals. These successors, known as the *diadochoi*, immediately fell into more than fifty years of war for control of territories within Alexander's empire. This period of conflict saw the birth of several new kingdoms and ushered in the Hellenistic age, with the Antigonids ruling in Macedonia and the Seleucids in Syria. More important for our purposes is the territory of Egypt, which quickly came under the rule of Ptolemy I, one of Alexander's most trusted generals.

Ptolemy was installed as ruler of Egypt by his army and later given the title "king" (Gk. *basileus*) in 304. A new Ptolemaic kingdom was formed, which—while not always stable—outstripped any previous Egyptian dynasty in both size and endurance, lasting over 270 years. The capital city of Alexandria became the most far-reaching international center of trade in the Mediterranean region and an important cultural and religious hub. The royal Ptolemaic administration was likewise sprawling and prosperous, offering tremendous social and economic opportunities and, unsurprisingly, attracting people from around the Mediterranean world.

1 For more details on this period, see Ian Worthington, *Ptolemy I: King and Pharaoh of Egypt* (Oxford: Oxford University Press, 2016); Günther Hölbl, *A History of the Ptolemaic Empire* (New York: Routledge, 2001); Katelijn Vandorpe, "The Ptolemaic Period," in *A Companion to Ancient Egypt*, ed. Alan B. Lloyd, BCAW (Malden, MA: Wiley-Blackwell, 2010); Graham Shipley, *The Greek World after Alexander: 323–30 BC* (London: Routledge, 2000).

Ptolemaic Egypt succeeded in large part because its Greek rulers managed to balance tradition and innovation on different levels. On the one hand, the kingdom was deliberately fashioned as a continuation of the ancient and sophisticated Egyptian civilization. That tradition mattered greatly to the majority population of native Egyptians, who now lived under Hellenistic rule. To maintain the goodwill of that population (and others), the Ptolemaic administration tended to stay out of more private matters. For example, the state exerted minimal influence in local customs, religious practice, and private legal proceedings, even providing a certain level of financial investment in these areas. But on the other hand, the kingdom was also deliberately Hellenistic in the realm of public life. Greeks were overtly favored within the Ptolemaic administration, with more economic privileges, access to political power, and sociocultural credibility in general.

As a result, the most prevalent distinction in Ptolemaic Egyptian life was between Greeks and non-Greeks. But as time went on, being "Greek" became more of a social and cultural identity rather than a strictly ethnic one. It is true that ethnic Greeks who had emigrated to Egypt were at the top of the social pecking order. But it was also possible for a Thracian or a Jew, for example, to *become* Greek in a certain sense by adopting the Greek ways of life that were deemed most important in private or public life (e.g., intermarriage with Greeks or military service). The way this social dynamic worked out in everyday life remains debated. But ultimately, it was the native Egyptians—who largely worshiped their own gods and observed their own cultural customs—who tended to have the lowest social status, since they were regarded as the least Greek.

One key characteristic of higher social status in Hellenistic Egypt was the increasing use of the Greek language throughout the population. Cultural change and language change often go hand in hand, but rarely do they occur quickly. Much of the early Ptolemaic administration occurred in the native Egyptian language, Demotic. But by the time of Ptolemy II, Greek was functionally the official language of Egypt. This shift was not enforced by the administration. But speaking Demotic had no expectations or incentives attached to it, while speaking Greek did.[2] So although the population of Hellenistic Egypt remained multilingual as a whole, anyone who wanted to avoid being marginalized in a Hellenized world and to take advantage of new economic opportunities was quick to learn Greek. One people group that did so was the Jewish community of Hellenistic Egypt.

The Jews of Hellenistic Egypt

According to the Old Testament, the history of the Jewish people in Egypt goes as far back as Abraham, Isaac, and Joseph (Gen. 12; 37).[3] Much of their history in later periods is connected with the movement of populations that occurred during the rise and fall of major empires. In 722 BC, the northern kingdom of Israel fell to the Assyrians, and the people were exiled (2 Kings 17). The southern kingdom of Judah met a similar fate in 586 BC, when it fell to the Babylonians, again leading to the exile and dispersion of the people (2 Kings 25), some of whom resettled in Egypt (Jer. 40–43).

---

2 Plutarch, *Anton.* 27.4.

3 For more detail on the Jews in Hellenistic Egypt, see Erich S. Gruen, *Diaspora: Jews amidst Greeks and Romans* (Cambridge, MA: Harvard University Press, 2002); Gruen, "Jews and Greeks," in *A Companion to the Hellenistic World*, ed. Andrew Erskine, BCAW (Malden, MA: Blackwell, 2006), 264–79; Joseph Mélèze Modrzejewski, "How to Be a Jew in Hellenistic Egypt?," in *Diasporas in Antiquity*, ed. Shaye J. D. Cohen and Ernest S. Frerichs, BJS 288 (Atlanta: Scholars Press, 1993), 65–91.

The eventual fall of the Babylonian Empire also allowed large-scale Jewish migration, not only back to Judea (Ezra 1) but eventually also to far-flung corners of the known world. Amid all the movement across the centuries of this diaspora ("scattering"), many Jews settled in Egypt, as ample evidence shows.[4]

The earliest nonbiblical evidence for Jewish presence in Egypt dates to the sixth century BC and comes from a military outpost and travel checkpoint called Elephantine, situated on an island in the Nile River.[5] But the Jewish presence in Egypt increased significantly in the Hellenistic period. Ptolemy I is reported to have led thousands of Jewish prisoners of war to Egypt after his victory over Judea in the late fourth century BC.[6] Others emigrated voluntarily to take advantage of economic opportunity or to escape ongoing conflicts between Hellenistic kingdoms in the second century.[7] Regardless of how they got there, huge numbers of Jews lived in Ptolemaic Egypt of their own accord. Josephus even reports that at a certain point, the size of the Jewish population in Alexandria was second only to that of Jerusalem itself.[8]

Jews in Hellenistic Egypt thrived in large measure because they faced virtually no social, economic, or cultural barriers. Since they were free to organize certain internal affairs related to religion and law, Jews remained distinct in various ways from the other groups

---

4 E.g., 1 Macc. 15:22–23; Josephus, *Ant.* 14.114–15; Philo, *Leg.* 281–83.
5 Whether and how to consider this community Jewish has long been a topic of debate given the many religious distinctives in Elephantine. See Joseph Mélèze Modrzejew-ski, *The Jews of Egypt: From Rameses II to Emperor Hadrian*, trans. Robert Cornman (Princeton, NJ: Princeton University Press, 1995), 21–98.
6 Let. Aris. 12–13.
7 1 Macc. 9:70–72; Josephus, *Ag. Ap.* 1.186–89; *Ant.* 13.337.
8 Josephus, *Ant.* 12.7–9.

around them. But those distinctions still allowed a kind of symbiosis with Hellenistic culture that did not seem to create tensions among the Jews themselves. In fact, from the perspective of Hellenistic culture at large, Jews were generally considered Greek "Hellenes," just like the other groups of Greek-speaking immigrants to Egypt.[9] As already noted, that status granted both upward social mobility and civic rights that were not otherwise available.[10]

As Hellenes, Jews worked in a variety of roles in agriculture, commerce, royal administration, and the military, where they could rise even to the rank of officer with all its privileges.[11] Jews occupied these roles not only in the capital city of Alexandria but also in the countryside. In addition, numerous sources attest the presence of prayerhouses (Gk. *proseuchai*) throughout Egypt. Several were dedicated in honor of both God and the Ptolemaic monarchy, the latter of which not only granted them official approval but also occasional sponsorship. One prayerhouse located southeast of Alexandria was dedicated (in Greek) in the second century BC as follows:

> On behalf of King Ptolemy and Queen Cleopatra, Ptolemy, the son of Epikydes, chief of police, and the Jews in Athribis [dedicate] this house of prayer to the Most High God.[12]

9 See Mélèze Modrzejewski, *Jews of Egypt*, 80–83.

10 This was especially so for native-born Egyptians, who were effectively regarded (and treated) as a peasant minority. Hellenes, however, were not as privileged as full, ethnic-Greek citizens of Alexandria, who were exempt from certain taxes.

11 Josephus, *Ag. Ap.* 1.200–204; *Ant.* 14.99, 131–32; 18.159; 20.147; Philo, *Legat.* 129; *Flacc.* 56–57; cf. 3 Macc. 3:10.

12 *Corpus Inscriptionum Judaicarum* 2.1443. Translation adapted from no. 27 in William Horbury and David Noy, eds., *Jewish Inscriptions of Graeco-Roman Egypt: With an Index of the Jewish Inscriptions of Egypt and Cyrenaica* (Cambridge: Cambridge University Press, 1992), 45.

With aspects of both traditional religion and contemporary culture in view, these institutions illustrate how Jewish life was simultaneously distinct from yet symbiotic with Hellenistic culture.

Participating in Hellenistic society in these ways meant that many Jews not only spoke Greek fluently but could also read and write it. Being considered a Hellene in Ptolemaic Egypt involved more than this but certainly not less. As it happens, writing in Greek is the best evidence for showing how the Jews were not socially isolated but part of the "bilingual middle sector" of Ptolemaic society.[13] Huge troves of ancient documents related to the everyday affairs of Hellenistic Jews—receipts, wills, private letters, and so on—display a range of facility in Greek composition and style. Numerous Jewish literary works in Greek also display considerable linguistic sophistication. Cumulatively, these sources attest to a Hellenistic Jewish community in Ptolemaic Egypt with the training, tools, resources, and habits for a thriving writing culture in Greek.[14]

The (Possible) Origins of the Greek Pentateuch

Understanding the social context of Hellenistic Judaism is essential to narrowing down the possibilities for why the Hebrew Bible was translated into Greek in the first place. Scholars agree that the first portion to be translated was the Pentateuch, probably in the mid-third century BC.[15] Given the importance of the Torah to Jewish life and

13 Marja Vierros, *Bilingual Notaries in Hellenistic Egypt: A Study of Greek as a Second Language* (Brussels: Koninklijke Vlaamse Academie van België voor Wetenschappen en Kunsten, 2012), 225–29.

14 Worthington, *Ptolemy I*, 103, 136, 189; Gruen, *Diaspora*, 68–69.

15 Scholars base this view on literary evidence such as the Prologue to Ben Sira, the discovery of second-century-BC manuscript evidence, and external linguistic evidence. See Emanuel Tov, *Textual Criticism of the Hebrew Bible*, 3rd ed. (Minneapolis:

practice, it is not all that surprising that it would be the top priority. While there is no unanimity on precisely what prompted the translation, we can outline several important contours in the discussion to highlight some likely scenarios.

Learning from Aristeas

The best-known explanation of why the Greek Pentateuch was produced is found in an ancient document called the Letter of Aristeas, likely dating to the mid-second century BC. This document is framed as an eyewitness account of events that purportedly occurred a century earlier in the Ptolemaic royal court.

In the Letter of Aristeas, we read that "the divine Law" of Moses (i.e., the Pentateuch) was translated at the request of Ptolemy II Philadelphus (r. 285–246 BC), whose librarian, Demetrius of Phalerum, wanted it for the king's renowned collections in Alexandria.[16] Aristeas himself persuaded the high priest of Jerusalem to arrange for the translation in return for the release of Jewish prisoners of war. Seventy-two translators were dispatched from the Jerusalem temple and arrived at Ptolemy's royal palace. At that point we read the following account:

> When they entered with the gifts which had been sent with them and the valuable parchments, on which the law was inscribed in gold in Jewish [i.e., Hebrew] characters—for the parchment was wonderfully prepared and the connection between the pages had been so effected as to be invisible—the king, as soon as he saw them,

---

Fortress, 2012), 114; John A. L. Lee, *A Lexical Study of the Septuagint Version of the Pentateuch*, SCS 14 (Chico, CA: Scholars Press, 1983).

16 Let. Aris. 3.

began to ask them about the books. And . . . he said: "I thank you, my friends, and I thank him that sent you still more, and most of all God, whose oracles these are."[17]

The translators were then welcomed with a seven-day feast and completed their task in seventy-two days. The translation was finished, praised by Ptolemy II, and deposited in the royal library with future revisions strictly forbidden (cf. Deut. 4:2).[18]

Scholars now regard the Letter of Aristeas as mostly, if not entirely, fictitious. Doubts about its authenticity surfaced in scholarship on Jerome's writing but grew in the seventeenth century and have only increased in light of historical errors and significant improbabilities in the account. For example, Demetrius of Phalerum was apparently never the Alexandrian librarian. Nor is it likely that Aristeas (a Gentile in the Ptolemaic court) would have had the kind of familiarity with Jewish practice that is on display in the Letter of Aristeas.

But even if it is partly fictitious, there are things we can learn from the Letter of Aristeas, as it highlights some of the underlying concerns of (at least some within) the Jewish community in Egypt. For

---

17 Let. Aris. 176–178 (cf. Josephus, *Ant.* 12.87–90), modified translation from R. H. Charles, ed., *The Apocrypha and Pseudepigrapha of the Old Testament in English*, 2 vols. (Oxford: Clarendon, 1913).

18 See Jennifer M. Dines, *The Septuagint*, UBW (London: T&T Clark, 2004), 27–39; James Carleton Paget, "The Origins of the Septuagint," in *The Jewish-Greek Tradition in Antiquity and the Byzantine Empire*, ed. James K. Aitken and James Carleton Paget (Cambridge: Cambridge University Press, 2014), 106–11; Benjamin G. Wright, "The Letter of Aristeas and the Question of Septuagint Origins Redux," *JAJ* 2, no. 3 (2011): 304–26. Other ancient writings contain accounts similar to or derived from the Letter of Aristeas, most notably Philo, *Mos.* 2.25–44; Josephus, *Ant.* 12.11–118; *Ag. Ap.* 2.45–47; and extracts attributed to Aristobulus, Demetrius the Chronographer, Ezekiel the Tragedian, and Artapanus in Eusebius, *Praep. ev.* 8–9, and Clement of Alexandria, *Strom.* 1.22.141, 150; 1.23.154, 155.

example, the Letter of Aristeas portrays King Ptolemy II as deferential toward the Jerusalem priesthood and sympathetic to the wisdom of the Mosaic law. Such a picture may suggest a desire to encourage loyalty among Jews in Egypt to both the Jerusalem priesthood and the Ptolemaic king, to justify the participation of educated Jews in a Hellenistic world, or to manage how other Hellenes perceived Jewish culture and heritage. Similarly, in its portrayal of the work of the seventy-two translators, the Letter of Aristeas echoes the story of the seventy elders present at Mount Sinai (Ex. 24), thereby lending credibility to the Greek Pentateuch as a divinely approved translation of Scripture that was clearly connected with the temple text.

If nothing else, the Letter of Aristeas certainly tells us that the Greek Pentateuch was produced by the late second century BC in Egypt and was regarded by (at least some) Hellenistic Jews as equal in authority to the Hebrew Bible precisely because it was viewed as a translation of the highest quality.

Considering External Motivations

Despite the historical inaccuracies and ulterior motives for the Letter of Aristeas, some scholars still believe that its most basic plot element can help explain the origins of the Greek Pentateuch. This perspective favors the idea that the translation was a result of motivations external to the Jewish community itself, specifically that some kind of official support or request came from the royal administration (and that it was perhaps destined for deposit in the library in Alexandria).[19]

19 Representative here are Dominique Barthélemy, "Pourquoi la Torah a-t-elle été traduite en Grec?," in *On Language, Culture, and Religion: In Honour of Eugene A. Nida*, ed. Matthew Black and William A. Smalley (Paris: Mouton, 1974), 32–41; Gilles Dorival, Marguerite Harl, and Olivier Munnich, *La Bible Greque des Septante:*

To be sure, it is hard to explain why the story of Hellenistic royal sponsorship would have arisen within Ptolemaic Judaism if it were totally fictional (especially if the translation were really a Jewish initiative). In reality, certain parts of the narrative of the Letter of Aristeas do fit into what we know of Ptolemaic Egyptian history, the Hellenistic cultural world, and the place of the Jews in it.

One important factor here is the context of vibrant scholarship that characterized Hellenistic Alexandria.[20] Beginning with Ptolemy I in 305 BC, the monarchy devoted major resources to developing a planned cultural policy, including the famous Library and Museum of Alexandria. Ptolemy's vision probably originated in his own education and was shared by his closest associates. For example, Ptolemy's personal confidant and former king, Alexander the Great, is known to have had a close relationship with Aristotle himself. In fact, according to the Greek historian Strabo,

Aristotle bequeathed his own library to [the peripatetic philosopher] Theophrastus, to whom he also left his school; and he is the first man, so far as I know, to have collected books and to have taught the kings in [Hellenistic] Egypt how to arrange a library.[21]

Du judaïsme hellénistique au christianisme ancien (Paris: Cerf, 1988), 72–78; Arie van der Kooij, "Perspectives on the Study of the Septuagint: Who Are the Translators?," in *Perspectives in the Study of the Old Testament and Judaism*, ed. Florentino García Martínez and Ed Noort, VTSup 73 (Leiden: Brill, 1998), 214–29; Natalio Fernández Marcos, "The Greek Pentateuch and the Scholarly Milieu of Alexandria," *SEC* 2 (2009): 81–89.

20 See Fausto Montana, "Hellenistic Scholarship," in *Brill's Companion to Ancient Greek Scholarship*, ed. Franco Montanari, Stephanos Matthaios, and Antonios Rengakos (Leiden: Brill, 2015), 60–183.

21 Strabo, *Geogr.* 13.608, trans. Horace Leonard Jones, LCL 223 (Cambridge, MA: Harvard University Press, 1969), 110–11.

To cultivate Alexandria as a city of learning, Ptolemy sought to persuade Greek intellectuals to move there. Among those who did was none other than Demetrius of Phalerum, a pupil of Theophrastus who not only appears in the Letter of Aristeas but is also said to have helped shape Ptolemy's cultural policies. Within this kind of intellectual context, it is natural to envision a translation like the Greek Pentateuch getting underway.

Another important factor that favors external motivations is the approach of the Ptolemaic administration to the legal system.[22] The monarchy went to some lengths to ensure that its proclamations were accessible to all its subjects by publishing new decrees in multiple languages. Not only that, but legal texts already in existence from non-Greek people groups were often translated into Greek.[23] That being the case, it would have been entirely consistent for the monarchy to have requested (or somehow supported) the translation of the Jewish legal tradition too, as the Letter of Aristeas claims.[24]

Considering Internal Motivations

Although there is some circumstantial evidence that external motivations influenced the production of the Greek Pentateuch, many scholars consider motivations internal to the Jewish community to be more important. It is worth pointing out, however, that the boundary

22 See Siegfried Kreuzer, "The Origins and Transmission of the Septuagint," in *Introduction to the LXX*, ed. Siegfried Kreuzer, trans. David A. Brenner and Peter Altmann (Waco, TX: Baylor University Press, 2019), 14–16.

23 E.g., P.Oxy. 46.3285 (TM 63672), a papyrus from the mid-second century AD, preserves the Greek translation of an Egyptian Demotic legal code, which was probably completed in the early Ptolemaic period.

24 At the same time, however, it is not clear how the Greek Pentateuch would have provided a practical body of legislative code for a community of socially engaged Hellenes like the Jews of Egypt.

line between internal and external is not always clear. Without discussing all the theories that have been proposed, we can synthesize some recent suggestions to fill in more details about the possible origins of the Greek Pentateuch.[25]

Perhaps the most obvious factor within Hellenistic Judaism in Egypt that must have motivated the translation of the Pentateuch was the early adoption of Greek, likely as a first language. This change would have posed certain challenges in religious life. As the Jewish community participated in a Greek-speaking world, its members increasingly lost touch with the Hebrew language in which their Scripture was written.[26] Since it is clear that Jewish worship usually involved reading Scripture, whether in public or private, it would have been a natural step to translate it into Greek.[27]

If this liturgical need within Egyptian Judaism prompted the production of the Greek Pentateuch, then that written project was probably preceded by oral translation. In the Hellenistic era, oral translation

25 See Natalio Fernández Marcos, *The Septuagint in Context: Introduction to the Greek Version of the Bible*, trans. Wilfred G. E. Watson, 2nd ed. (Leiden: Brill, 2000), 53–66; Carleton Paget, "Origins," 111–19. The synthesis here draws on James K. Aitken, "The Origins and Social Context of the Septuagint," in *T&T Clark Handbook of Septuagint Research*, ed. William A. Ross and W. Edward Glenny (London: Bloomsbury T&T Clark, 2021), 9–20; John A. L. Lee, *The Greek of the Pentateuch: Grinfield Lectures on the Septuagint, 2011–2012* (Oxford: Oxford University Press, 2018), esp. 173–209; Anneli Aejmelaeus, "The Septuagint and Oral Translation," in *XIV Congress of the International Organization for Septuagint and Cognate Studies, Helsinki, 2010*, ed. Melvin K. H. Peters, SCS 59 (Atlanta: SBL, 2013), 5–13.

26 Even in Jerusalem and its vicinities—where Jews had spoken Aramaic for generations—Greek was making major inroads.

27 See, e.g., Ex. 13:14–15; Deut. 4:9; 6:6–9; 31:10–13; cf. Neh. 8:7–8; Philo, *Somn.* 2.127. The theory of liturgical origins was originally proposed by Henry St. John Thackeray, *The Septuagint and Jewish Worship: A Study in Origins* (London: Oxford University Press, 1921).

would have occurred in Greek, but in the earlier period of Persian rule, it would have occurred in Aramaic. Various scholars have suggested that this oral translation may have been extemporaneous at first, with minimal coordination or effort to write things down. But over time certain translation practices developed that became conventional, perhaps especially within public places of worship.

Some of the best evidence for the theory of oral translation preceding written translation comes from the Greek Pentateuch itself. Within the five translated books, we find many cases in which specific Greek words are used consistently to render specific Hebrew words. That is especially the case when important theological concepts are involved. For example, the Hebrew term for "covenant" (*berith*) is almost always translated with the Greek *diathēkē*, "righteousness" (Heb. *tsedakah*) with *dikaiosynē* (Gk.), and the word for "law" (Heb. *torah*) with *nomos* (Gk.). Beyond these examples, many other nontheological words and grammatical features were also handled consistently in translation almost every time they appeared, likely because they occur so frequently in the Hebrew text.

The Greek Pentateuch also provides glimpses of the use of Aramaic in oral translation, which was carried over into a kind of Greek form. A good example is the word for "the Passover." In Hebrew, the word for "the Passover" is *happasakh* (with "the" attached to the beginning), but in Aramaic it is *paskha* (with "the" attached to the end). Interestingly, in the course of their work, whenever the translators of the Pentateuch came to the Hebrew word *happasakh*, they wrote down the Aramaic word *paskha* but using Greek letters (πάσχα, *pascha*).[28] This decision

---

28 Greek students may recognize τὸ πάσχα as a vocabulary word they learned for "the Passover" without realizing its Aramaic origins and connection with the Greek Old Testament.

suggests that by the time the Greek Pentateuch was produced, the Greek version of the Aramaic word for "the Passover" was so familiar from use within the Jewish community that it was considered a suitable translation of Hebrew. These kinds of features of the translation itself provide good evidence that over time—prior to producing the written translation—the Jewish community in Egypt had developed some generally accepted translation practices.

Recent scholarship has also shed light on the question of origins by considering the translators themselves and the context of their work. Although it has become common to assert that the translation of the Hebrew Bible into Greek was unique or unprecedented, in reality that is not entirely correct. Yes, the Greek Pentateuch was the first written translation of Scripture. But Egyptian Jews lived in a multilingual world. So the task of translation itself was not unusual, a reality attested by huge quantities of ancient documentary evidence. The Greek Pentateuch should therefore be understood squarely within this broader context of translation activity. In fact, there are numerous parallels between the translation strategies in the Greek Pentateuch and those in official documents of the Ptolemaic administration. These parallels suggest that the translators of the Greek Pentateuch might have been professionally trained (or might have consulted with those who were).[29]

These observations help highlight how, once the Jewish translators of the Greek Pentateuch sat down to their task, it was an intentional and coherent group project with important precedents.

---

29 See James K. Aitken, "The Septuagint and Egyptian Translation Methods," in *XV Congress of the International Organization for Septuagint and Cognate Studies, Munich, 2013*, ed. Wolfgang Kraus, Michaël N. van der Meer, and Martin Meiser (Atlanta: SBL, 2016), 269–93.

It is distinctly *not* the case that the translators were improvising as they went along—word by word and clause by clause—bumping into things in the text that they may not have anticipated or known how to handle. They certainly faced challenges. But their work was informed by existing practices within the Jewish community and strategies typical within the broader social context of Hellenistic Egypt.

Summary

Stepping back, we can see how it is unlikely that the Greek Pentateuch was prompted by a single, identifiable factor either outside or inside early Hellenistic Judaism itself. The project was motivated by a number of interconnected needs, opportunities, and desires in and around the Jewish community.

On the one hand, given the relationship between the Ptolemaic monarchy and Jewish community, we should not rule out some manner of external support for the translation initiative, even if it was indirect. Any such support was probably not as grandiose as the Letter of Aristeas suggests. But the time and physical resources needed to complete the project would have involved considerable financial burdens. Any royal sponsorship of Jewish religious life in general could have been collectively allocated to the organization and execution of the written translation.

On the other hand, aside from financial coordination among the Jewish community to support the project, the translators must have cooperated with religious leadership, if they were not already part of it. If nothing else, this cooperation was necessary for them to gain access to the Hebrew scrolls used as the basis of their work. Since those scrolls contained unpointed Hebrew (whch mns tht th wrds hd n vwls jst lk ths),[30] the translators may have benefited from some kind of official guidance or oversight to help with the more challenging aspects of their work.

The Origins of Other Jewish Books in Greek

What about the origins of the rest of the Greek Old Testament? Unfortunately, we have even less to go on here than with the Greek Pentateuch. There are no ancient accounts like the Letter of Aristeas for the other books. And although several criteria could be used to date the translation of the other books, none are conclusive.

First, in terms of location, it is uncertain that the other books of the Greek Old Testament were produced in Egypt, as the Pentateuch was. In general, scholars take Egypt to be the default location for Jewish translations of Scripture, but most recognize that at least some of that activity occurred in Palestine, though just how much is debated.[31]

Second, in terms of timing, most scholars continue to follow the basic conclusion, first presented by Gilles Dorival,[32] that the rest of the books of the Hebrew Bible (and Apocrypha) were translated or composed between the mid-third century BC and the first or second century AD. But scholarly proposals differ widely on their exact dating and order. Dorival suggests that the books that followed most closely after the translation of the Pentateuch were (in no particular order) Psalms, Isaiah, Jeremiah, Ezekiel, the Minor Prophets, Joshua, Judges,

---

30 Hebrew vowels go *around* the consonants, but they were not added to the written text until the medieval period. As the example shows, a vowelless English phrase is usually easy to understand but sometimes leaves room for ambiguity.

31 See Emanuel Tov, "Some Reflections on the Hebrew Texts from Which the Septuagint Was Translated," *JNSL* 19 (1993): 107–22.

32 Gilles Dorival, "L'achèvement de la Septante dans le judaïsme: De la faveur au rejet," in Dorival, Harl, and Munnich, *La Bible Greque des Septante*, 111.

Chronicles, and Kingdoms (i.e., 1 Samuel–2 Kings). Some or all of those were probably being translated or written simultaneously in the early second century BC. These may have then been followed by Daniel, Job, Proverbs, and Esther sometime in the first century BC, leaving books such as Ruth, Lamentations, Song of Songs, Ecclesiastes, and Ezra–Nehemiah until sometime after the turn of the era.[33]

Many details of Dorival's survey have been questioned or refined over the years, with some scholars significantly shrinking the window of time in which the canonical books were translated. But doing so may result from unrealistic or anachronistic assumptions about Jewish literary priorities, given that other noncanonical Jewish Greek writings began appearing in the same time frame, including some in the second century BC (e.g., 1–2 Maccabees, Sirach, Baruch, Tobit, Judith) and some over the next two centuries (e.g., 3–4 Maccabees, additions to Esther, Psalms of Solomon).[34]

Concluding Thoughts

One important point here is that the Jewish community in the Hellenistic and early Roman periods fostered a vibrant Greek literary tradition in both Egypt and Palestine, including Greek translations of the Old Testament books as well as other Greek writings (both translations and original compositions). Additionally, as we discuss in chapter 4, almost as soon as the earlier books of the Hebrew Bible were translated, they were revised or even redone from scratch. No

---

33 See Dines, *Septuagint*, 45–47.

34 See James K. Aitken, "The Septuagint and Jewish Translation Traditions," in *Septuagint, Targum and Beyond: Comparing Aramaic and Greek Versions from Jewish Antiquity*, ed. David James Shepherd, Jan Joosten, and Michaël N. van der Meer, JSJSup 193 (Leiden: Brill, 2019), 208–10.

single part of this Jewish Greek literary activity can be fully understood if isolated from the rest or from the broader environment of Greek writings in general.

All things considered, many open questions remain concerning the origins of the Greek Old Testament. Matters of motivation, translator identity, timing, and location remain partly, if not entirely, uncertain. As a result, scholars have increasingly relied on closer analysis of the Greek language itself to help clarify these topics and understand the style and character of the translation. These issues occupy our attention in the next chapter.

3

How Was the Greek Old Testament Translated?

THE QUESTION POSED BY THE TITLE of this chapter seems simple. But answering it has proved to be one of the most challenging issues within all Septuagint scholarship. Part of the reason for the difficulty is that there is no good way to describe the translation of the entire Greek Old Testament all at once. It is like trying to describe the color you might see inside a box of crayons (as if there is just one)—only to open it up and find some scented markers mixed in too.

Some shared features, however, can be identified across the entire Greek Old Testament. At a general level—so general it might be un-helpful—we can say that the majority of the Greek translations of the Old Testament adhere to the word order of their source text and also clearly convey its meaning in conventional, postclassical ("Koine") Greek.[1] But there is more to say, including qualifications and exceptions to that description.

---

1   The term *postclassical* is preferable to the more traditional *Koine*, which tends to be portrayed within biblical scholarship as a kind of colloquial subvariety of "Greek,"

To understand the translation approaches in the Greek Old Testament, we will progress in three stages:

1. Untangling language from translation: Why and how should matters of language itself be kept distinct from decisions involved in translation?
2. Translating the Pentateuch: What are the key characteristics of the Greek Pentateuch as a translation, and what kinds of linguistic features did they produce?
3. Producing other Jewish books in Greek: How and why did the later translation of other books of the Greek Old Testament differ from the Greek Pentateuch?

These steps help illustrate the diversity and sophistication of the language of the Greek Old Testament, showing that there was no singular or predictable approach to translation.[2]

Untangling Language from Translation

Imagine that every book in your copy of the Old Testament was translated by different people, in different places, for different audiences, with different goals, over the course of about four centuries.[3] It would be a cross section of approaches to translation *and* a tapestry of language varieties. Each translation would have been made with

---

which is incorrect. See further William A. Ross, "Some Problems with Talking about 'Septuagint Greek,'" *JSJ* (forthcoming).

2 For discussions of the translation of each Old Testament book, see James K. Aitken, ed., *T&T Clark Companion to the Septuagint* (London: T&T Clark, 2015); Siegfried Kreuzer, ed., *Introduction to the LXX*, trans. David A. Brenner and Peter Altmann (Waco, TX: Baylor University Press, 2019).

3 We could also add "from source texts of varying quality" (see chap. 5).

assumptions about how to understand the original, how to communicate it in English, and what the expected readers want.

That is a picture of what we have in the Greek Old Testament. But within Septuagint scholarship, the study of translation has at times been conflated with matters of language itself. Translation obviously involves language, but the two can and should be distinguished. *Translation* involves decisions about how to convert one language into another. *Language* involves decisions about how to communicate with others in a way they can understand and perhaps even appreciate. To illustrate, consider the New Testament examples in table 3.1.

Table 3.1   Translation Possibilities for John 1:12

KJV	But as many as received him, to them gave he power to become the sons of God, even to them that believe on his name.
ESV	But to all who did receive him, who believed in his name, he gave the right to become children of God.
TCEB	Some welcomed him into their lives and believed in him. He gave those people the right to become God's children.

Each translation does things differently. The King James Version feels quite traditional, perhaps to the point that it may sound a little odd. Comparatively, the English Standard Version is less formal but still sounds educated, with differences in word order and vocabulary choice. When compared with the other two, the Casual English Bible (TCEB) sounds conversational yet might be the easiest to understand.

Whatever we might say about which of these translations is "best" or "most accurate," it is important to acknowledge three things:

- *None* represent the meaning or grammar of the underlying Greek perfectly.
- *None* avoid making interpretive decisions for the reader.
- *All* communicate effectively in English, even though they each say something similar but in different ways and with different stylistic choices and levels of formality.

The first and second points are true of all translations because no two languages work precisely the same way, so translation always involves some mismatch. But the third point is true because *language* is distinct from *translation*.

In other words, there is more than one way of saying the same thing, and there are many potential motivations for choosing one way over another. For the process of translation, those choices and motivations are influenced by factors beyond the source text itself. Those factors include preference in spelling and punctuation, conventions of comprehensible usage, level of education, and social expectations for style, clarity, and formality. Because these factors are linguistic in nature, they are pertinent to *every* approach to translation.

Unfortunately, Septuagint scholars do not always distinguish language from translation. This tendency began over a century ago when Henry St. John Thackeray classified books in the Greek Old Testament corpus with one of three labels: "good" Greek, "indifferent" Greek, or "literal or unintelligent versions."[4] These labels are problematic because they imply that the more "literal" the approach to *translation*, the less "intelligent" the outcome in *language*. Such reasoning assumes that close adherence to the word order of a source text is always at odds

---

4 Henry St. J. Thackeray, *A Grammar of the Old Testament in Greek according to the Septuagint* (Cambridge: Cambridge University Press, 1909), 1:12–16.

with conventional or stylish translation results, which is untrue.[5] It also assumes that there is sufficient evidence (or warrant) to judge what constitutes superior or inferior Greek, which is also untrue. Such assumptions can lead to flawed conclusions about the nature of translation in the Greek Old Testament and the practices of ancient Jews who produced it, as explored further below.[6]

Translating the Pentateuch

As discussèd in chapter 2, the Pentateuch was likely the first portion translated into Greek. Consequently, it became a model for later translation activity and therefore occupies most of our attention in this chapter.

We can evaluate the major translation characteristics of the Greek Pentateuch using three categories related to language conventions.[7] From a linguistic perspective, for an expression to be conventional it has to be comprehensible and sound appropriate to other speakers of

---

5 Even so, this logic has been influential within Septuagint scholarship. As a more recent example, Raija Sollamo states that some translators of the Greek Old Testament "strive for as *literal* a translation as possible; others favor idiomatic language and *good* Greek style." "The Study of Translation Technique," in *Die Sprache der Septuaginta / The Language of the Septuagint*, ed. Eberhard Bons and Jan Joosten, LXX.H 3 (Gütersloh: Gütersloher Verlagshaus, 2016), 165; emphasis added.

6 Detailed discussion of these issues can be found in James K. Aitken, "The Language of the Septuagint and Jewish-Greek Identity," in *The Jewish-Greek Tradition in Antiquity and the Byzantine Empire*, ed. James K. Aitken and James Carleton Padget (Cambridge: Cambridge University Press, 2014), 120–34; Aitken, "Outlook," in *The Reception of Septuagint Words in Jewish-Hellenistic and Christian Literature*, ed. Eberhard Bons, Ralph Brucker, and Jan Joosten, WUNT, 2nd ser., vol. 367 (Tübingen: Mohr Siebeck, 2014), 184–94; Ross, "Some Problems."

7 These categories build on John A. L. Lee, "Back to the Question of Greek Idiom," in *The Legacy of Soisalon-Soininen: Towards a Syntax of Septuagint Greek*, ed. Tuukka Kauhanen and Hanna Vanonen (Göttingen: Vandenhoeck & Ruprecht, 2020), 13–25. The examples provided below are limited and illustrative. Translations are our own.

a language.[8] As we discuss each category, we strive to keep the task of translation and the issue of language distinct but in close conversation.

Matching Hebrew Wording in Conventional Greek

As a general rule, the translators of the Pentateuch used conventional Greek to represent the Hebrew text word for word. Consider this example from Exodus 14:1, where each Hebrew word is matched in Greek and in the same order:

Hebrew:	*waydabber*	*yhwh*	*'elmoshe*	*le'mor*
Greek:	*kai elalēsen*	*kyrios*	*pros Mōusēn*	*legōn*
English:	Then spoke	the Lord	to Moses	saying

The approach to translation in this short verse is by far the most common. It is the prevailing characteristic of the Greek Pentateuch, and it was intentional. It produced several common features.

PARATAXIS

Hebrew narrative tends to move along by connecting clauses with a simple coordinating conjunction—"and" or "then" (Heb. *waw*)—which is called parataxis. For example, Genesis 1:3–5 reads, "*And* God said . . . *and* there was light. *And* God saw. . . . *And* God separated. . . . *And* God called. . . . *And* there was evening . . . ," and so on. Because Hebrew narrative does this so often and because the translators tended to represent each Hebrew word in Greek, parataxis is also common in the Greek Pentateuch, with the same type of conjunction (Gk. *kai*) appearing regularly.

---

8 See Joan Bybee, *Language, Usage and Cognition* (Cambridge: Cambridge University Press, 2010), 14–56, esp. 34–37.

RESUMPTIVE PRONOUN

In Hebrew it is not uncommon to find a sentence like this: "Take your sandals off your feet, for the place that you are standing on *it* is holy ground" (Ex. 3:5, our trans.) The "it" is called a resumptive pronoun and seems unnecessary from an English perspective, so most translations leave it out. But because the translators typically reproduced the Hebrew text word for word, the Greek Pentateuch also contains many resumptive pronouns, even though they are not common in other Greek writings.

REPORTED SPEECH MARKER

Biblical Hebrew has no punctuation marks as we think of them. To introduce reported speech, a writer would use a specific verb form that serves a similar purpose as quotation marks. For example, "All the Egyptians came to Joseph, *saying* [Heb. *le'mor*], 'Give us food!'" (Gen. 47:15, our trans.). Once again, the translators usually matched this Hebrew word with a corresponding Greek verb form for "saying" (Gk. *legōn*) or "answering" (Gk. *apokritheis*).

The majority of the Greek Pentateuch consists of translation like this, because Hebrew meaning and word order could typically be conveyed using conventional Greek. But the features chosen for discussion here are also noteworthy because they are *far more common* in Hebrew than in Greek. Because the translators approached their work so consistently, the features appear in the Greek Pentateuch with greater frequency than they probably would have in everyday conversation. That difference in frequency would have lent a distinctive sound to their work—a kind of stylistic enhancement from the source text—but without detracting from the intelligibility of the Greek translation.

Departing from Hebrew Wording in Conventional Greek

The next most common characteristic of the Greek Pentateuch is for the translation to depart from the Hebrew text in some way but still use conventional Greek.[9] There are three main reasons for this departure.[10]

LINGUISTIC MISMATCH

Hebrew and Greek work differently as languages. Sometimes the conventions for saying something in one language make it impossible to match another language word for word. Often this mismatch exists at basic levels of the language. It rarely affects meaning and, because it is difficult (if not impossible) to avoid, should be considered unintentional. Here are two examples:

Differing letters and sounds. Hebrew and Greek have differences in what sounds are used and how those sounds are represented in writing. When the translators came across proper nouns—the names of people or places—and wanted to transcribe them into

---

9 We assume here for the sake of discussion that the Greek translators were looking at a Hebrew text that agrees with the Masoretic Text, which is used as the basis of English Bibles. The possibility always exists that where the Greek translation *does not* match the Masoretic Text, it is because the translator's Hebrew text itself was different from the Masoretic Text, and the translator simply rendered it accordingly. See Karen H. Jobes and Moisés Silva, *Invitation to the Septuagint*, 2nd ed. (Grand Rapids, MI: Baker Academic, 2015), 164–71.

10 Note that a translation decision might be motivated by more than one of these three reasons at once. For extensive discussion of this characteristic, see John A. L. Lee, *The Greek of the Pentateuch: Grinfield Lectures on the Septuagint, 2011–2012* (Oxford: Oxford University Press, 2018).

Greek, they sometimes had to compromise. For example, while Hebrew has several letters that all represent slightly different variations of an *s* sound (שׁ שׂ ס צ), Greek has only one letter (σ). So the translator of Genesis had to use that Greek letter in the transcription of both the name *Shem* (שׁ) and the name *Sarai* (שׂ), despite the difference in sound.

Differing grammatical features. Hebrew has many grammatical features that Greek does not have (and vice versa). For example, Hebrew has a singular and a plural form for nouns, as well as a dual form for pairs. So the translators had to represent that dual form using a Greek plural form, which is less specific. Unlike Greek, Hebrew also has a directional suffix that can be added to nouns (meaning something like "toward *x*"), so the translators conveyed the meaning by adding a preposition in Greek where there is none in their Hebrew source text.

We could provide more examples.[11] For each instance the departure from the Hebrew text in translation, even if minor, was motivated by the desire to use conventional Greek language.

LINGUISTIC CHOICE

Because there is more than one way of saying the same thing, a speaker will choose from among different possibilities, some of which will seem equally appropriate and conventional. Two broad factors influence how someone chooses to say something one way and not another. First, choices are affected by cultural expectations created by the situation in which language is used—this factor is known as *register*. For example, language expectations are casual and spontaneous

---

11 See Takamitsu Muraoka, "Limitations of Greek in Representing Hebrew," in Bons and Joosten, *Die Sprache der Septuaginta / Language of the Septuagint*, 129–38.

when we speak to our children or send a text to a friend but become more formal and standardized when we speak to our boss or write a journal article. Second, choices are affected by individual aesthetic preferences—this factor is known as *style*.[12]

These two factors involved in linguistic choice prompted the translators of the Pentateuch to depart from the Hebrew wording, but it rarely altered the meaning in a significant way. Usually such departures conveyed meaning in a way that the translators felt was appropriate for their expected readership. Here are two kinds of linguistic choice.

Lexical variation. Often the translators of the Greek Pentateuch used the same Greek word each time they encountered a given Hebrew word. But sometimes they chose different Greek words to translate the same Hebrew word in different contexts. Some might categorize this translation approach as "mismatch" in translation since it is not perfectly consistent. But to do so is to overlook how lexical variation arises from matters of register and style.

As an example of register, the Hebrew verb "to command" (*tsavah*) was often translated with the Greek verbs *entellōmai* and *syntassō* but never with the verb *keleuō*, despite the fact that *keleuō* was quite common at the time. All three of these verbs convey very similar meanings. Why choose one over another? The answer is register. In the Pentateuch, it is usually an authority figure such as God, Moses, or Pharaoh who is commanding others. So the translators chose Greek verbs that suited the dignity of elevated social status and respect.[13]

---

12 See Douglas Biber and Susan Conrad, *Register, Genre and Style*, CTL (Cambridge: Cambridge University Press, 2009), 1–26.

13 See also John A. L. Lee, "'Εξαποστέλλω," in *Voces Biblicae: Septuagint Greek and Its Significance for the New Testament*, ed. Jan Joosten and Peter J. Tomson, CBET 49 (Leuven: Peeters, 2007), 99–113. Lee discusses how matters related to register in the Greek Pentateuch influenced New Testament authors.

As an example of style, there are several Hebrew prepositions that mean "before" or "in front of" (*liphney, beeyney, leeyney*), and we find varying preferences among the translators for prepositions used to render them into Greek. In Genesis and Exodus, we find the Greek word *enantion*, but in the other three books we find *enanti*, both of which are close in meaning. Why choose one over another? The answer is style—or perhaps even personal taste.[14]

Greek idiom. Frequently the translators chose to use expressions unique to Greek that departed from the Hebrew wording, despite the fact that other options existed that would have maintained the Hebrew wording. For example, in Greek some connecting words such as "so" (*de*) or "for" (*gar*) always take the second syntactical position in a clause (postpositive). So using these words in translation required deviating from Hebrew word order, even though other (i.e., nonpostpositive) options existed that would have preserved the word order (e.g., Gk. *kai, hoti*).[15]

CLARITY

The third reason for departing from the Hebrew text using conventional Greek was to maximize communicative clarity for the reader. In this kind of situation, *clarity* means clarity in the opinion of the translators themselves, which is not very different from interpreting something for a reader. This happened in many different ways.[16]

---

14 See Lee, *Greek of the Pentateuch*, 43–46.

15 The rationale for this approach is discussed below. Similarly, certain Greek words— such as *tis* ("a certain one") and *an* (to add contingency)—were common in more refined communication but not strictly necessary, and they do not have Hebrew counterparts. Using such words implies formal education in Greek and a willingness to use it without prompting from the Hebrew text, thus departing from its wording. See Lee, *Greek of the Pentateuch*, 92–110, 128–39.

16 In chap. 5, we also discuss the ways that theological beliefs occasionally prompted the translators to depart from their source text.

Pronoun substitution. Sometimes when there was a pronoun in the Hebrew text, a translator substituted a proper noun to minimize ambiguity as to what is happening to whom. For example, Genesis 37:35 ends with a comment about Jacob weeping for Joseph. The next verse says, "The Midianites sold *him* [Heb. *'oto*] in Egypt" (Gen. 37:36). But the Greek translator made a change: "The Midianites sold *Joseph* in Egypt." The pronoun "him" in Hebrew was substituted with the name "Joseph" in Greek to avoid confusion about who was sold.

Contemporization. Occasionally the Pentateuch translators used socioculturally specific language to help their readers understand the biblical text in terms familiar from everyday life. For example, in preparation for the coming famine, we find Joseph advising Pharaoh to appoint not just "overseers" of a general kind but *toparchas* (Gk., Gen. 41:34). In Ptolemaic Egypt, a *toparchēs* was an official in agricultural and economic administration, making the word a suitable choice by the translator for the narrative context within his contemporary social setting. Similarly, in Genesis 21:33, we find Abraham planting not a "tamarisk tree," as in the Hebrew, but an *aroura*, a Greek term known within Egypt for a plot of a specific size. The Greek Pentateuch also contains Egyptian loanwords, such as the floating container (Gk. *thibis*) in which baby Moses is found (Ex. 2:3).[17] All these choices represent a departure from the Hebrew in the sense that they are more culturally specific than strictly necessary, meant to clarify the text for an Egyptian readership.

Discourse markers. Many connecting words function as discourse markers that help structure the flow of thought into chunks in a way that facilitates comprehension. The desire for this sort of clarity motivated the choice to use postpositive connecting words like *de* ("and"), which

---

17 James K. Aitken, *No Stone Unturned: Greek Inscriptions and Septuagint Vocabulary*, CrSHB 5 (Winona Lake, IN: Eisenbrauns, 2014), 13–15.

departed from Hebrew word order, rather than another option like *kai* ("and"), which would have preserved it. So the translators themselves understood the development of thought in their Hebrew text at a high level and chose to follow Greek conventions to convey it well, even though that decision sometimes entailed departing from Hebrew word order.[18]

In short, the Pentateuch translators often had several reasons (and options) for deviating from a word-for-word adherence to their Hebrew text while still using conventional Greek.

Matching Hebrew Wording in Unconventional Greek

The final and least common characteristic of the Greek Pentateuch is that the translation sometimes matches the Hebrew wording in a way that may have sounded unconventional to Greek speakers.[19] Because this category is interesting to most Septuagint scholars, it gets a lot of attention. But this practice is, in fact, the exception and not the rule. It is motivated by two main factors.

REPLICATING HEBREW SYNTAX

As already discussed, following Hebrew word order in Greek typically allows using completely conventional Greek—but not always, as in the following examples.

18 See Christopher J. Fresch, "The Septuagint and Discourse Grammar," in *T&T Clark Handbook of Septuagint Research*, ed. William A. Ross and W. Edward Glenny (London: Bloomsbury T&T Clark, 2021), 79–92.

19 Our knowledge of what could have been considered "conventional" is partial and contingent on thorough analysis of whatever written texts have survived, which provide only an incomplete picture of the Greek language as a whole. It is also important to recognize that any new feature in language is unconventional at first but may become conventional if it is adopted in the language community. As we discuss in chap. 6, some new (and thus initially unconventional) linguistic features in the Greek Old Testament caught on in a way that influenced the language of New Testament authors—and perhaps even wider usage.

Distributives. In Hebrew the idea of distribution is expressed by repeating a word twice in a row. For example, the phrase "a man a man" means "each man" (Heb. *ish ish*, Ex. 36:4), and "a little a little" means "little by little" (Heb. *me'at me'at*, Ex. 23:30). When the translators reproduced each word of these phrases in Greek, the result was unconventional and probably would have slightly puzzled most Greek speakers.

Hebrew figures of speech. In English we say, "Don't let the cat out of the bag," when we want someone to keep a secret. But translating the *wording* of such idioms into another language does not preserve the *meaning*, since the meaning is culturally embedded. This same phenomenon affected the Greek Pentateuch. One Hebrew idiom common in texts discussing priestly activity is "to fill the hands," which essentially means "to ordain." But the translators rendered this Hebrew idiom word for word into Greek (e.g., Ex. 32:29; Lev. 8:33), resulting in "fill the hand" phrases that would have sounded as odd to ancient readers as the English translation does to us.

LEXICAL CONSISTENCY

As mentioned above, often the translators used the same Greek word in translation each time they encountered a given Hebrew word. At times this approach put Greek words to work doing things they had never done before, which would have sounded unconventional (at least at first). For example, the Hebrew word for "sea" (*yam*) could also refer to the "west," since the Mediterranean Sea lay in that direction from Israel. Whenever the translators encountered *yam* in the course of their work, they typically rendered it using the Greek word for "sea" (*thalassa*), even when the Hebrew was clearly referring to the "west" (e.g., Gen. 12:8). Because we have no evidence that this Greek word could also mean "west," it is reasonable to conclude that the resulting language in translation would have sounded unconventional—particularly since in Egypt the Mediterranean lies to the north!

Summary

Scholars generally agree that each book of the Pentateuch was translated by a different person. But recent research suggests that—in addition to whatever oral translation traditions had been established before the endeavor formally began—the translators collaborated as a group. Overall, those translators approached their task in a careful and balanced way, generally representing the Hebrew text in order at a word-for-word level in conventional Greek, though not without exceptions.

As the translators worked, their level of language was varied and eclectic, typically straightforward and unpretentious but not without formality, creativity, and the occasional literary flair. The translators demonstrate control of the Greek language consistent with intermediate Hellenistic education. Yet they also felt free to use the Greek language in certain new and stylized ways, which would have lent their work a distinctive sound. All told, the production of the Greek Pentateuch was a significant literary achievement.[20]

Producing Other Jewish Books in Greek

Given the enduring importance of the five books of Moses as a religious text within Judaism, it is no surprise that the Greek Pentateuch became

---

20 At the same time, we must remember that this was a multilingual environment in which translation was an everyday activity for most people, professionals or not. With experienced translators and a collaborative approach, the Greek Pentateuch could have been completed in as little as four months. See Lee, *Greek of the Pentateuch*, 173–209.

a benchmark for scriptural translation that would endure for centuries. Many—perhaps most—subsequent works strove to imitate it in certain ways, though some intentionally took a distinct approach. This section briefly explores how three broad traditions of translating other books of the Greek Old Testament compare to the Greek Pentateuch.

The Pentateuchal Tradition

Numerous other Jewish works imitate the style of the Greek Pentateuch. The translators of many biblical books like the Psalms and the Minor Prophets continued key aspects of that tradition (though there is debate over precisely how this unfolded).[21] In general, their approach sought to preserve meaning and word order in Greek, using much of the same standardized vocabulary choices from the Greek Pentateuch. They did this not only with fairly obvious equivalents but also with more technical terminology and rare words.[22]

In addition, many later translators imitated how the Greek Pentateuch dealt with certain aspects of Hebrew syntax, at times using rare but nevertheless conventional Greek.[23] At an even broader level, where the Pentateuch shared ideas or phrases with other biblical books,

21 See, for example, James Barr, "Did the Greek Pentateuch Really Serve as a Dictionary for the Translation of the Later Books?," in *Hamlet on a Hill: Semitic and Greek Studies Presented to T. Muraoka on the Occasion of His Sixty-Fifth Birthday*, ed. M. F. J. Baasten and W. Th. van Peursen, OLA 118 (Leuven: Peeters, 2003), 523–43.

22 Emanuel Tov, "The Impact of the Septuagint Translation of the Torah on the Translation of the Other Books," in *The Greek and Hebrew Bible: Collected Essays on the Septuagint*, VTSup 72 (Leiden: Brill, 1999), 184–91.

23 See William A. Ross, "The Septuagint as a Catalyst for Language Change in the Koine: A Usage-Based Approach," in *Die Septuaginta—Geschichte, Wirkung, Relevanz: 6. Internationale Fachtagung Veranstaltet von Septuaginta-Deutsch (LXX.D)*, ed. Martin Meiser, Michaela Geiger, Siegfried Kreuzer, and Marcus Sigismund, WUNT, 2nd ser., vol. 405 (Tübingen: Mohr Siebeck, 2018), 383–97; Aitken, "Language of the Septuagint," 127–28.

later translators imitated the wording of the Greek Pentateuch, likely because they knew it by heart and esteemed it.[24]

Of course, even amid the continuities in this tradition there is some variation, innovation, and distinct stylistic choices.[25] But by the late second century BC, the translator of Sirach could imply in his prologue that his approach imitated that taken in "the Law itself and the Prophets and the rest of the books," assuming his readers would know what he meant. So well accepted was the Pentateuchal tradition that it formed the basis of a kind of literary tradition within the broader Hellenistic world, with aspects of its linguistic style employed even by Jewish authors writing directly in Greek rather than translating from Hebrew (e.g., Ezekiel the Tragedian, Wisdom of Solomon, and perhaps Judith).[26]

The Paraphrastic Tradition

Not all translators sought to adhere to their Hebrew source text word for word as the default strategy, as the Pentateuchal tradition did. Another approach appeared within the Jewish community as early as the second century BC, in which translators were markedly less concerned to represent each word in order with a close equivalent. Notable examples of this paraphrastic tradition are the books of Proverbs, Job, 1–2 Chronicles, and Isaiah.

24 William A. Ross, "Style and Familiarity in Judges 19,7 (Old Greek): Establishing Dependence within the Septuagint," *Bib* 98, no. 1 (2017): 25–36; Myrto Theocharous, *Lexical Dependence and Intertextual Allusion in the Septuagint of the Twelve Prophets: Studies in Hosea, Amos and Micah*, LHBOTS 570 (London: T&T Clark, 2012).

25 See Jennifer M. Dines, "Was the LXX Pentateuch a Style-Setter for LXX Minor Prophets?," in *XIV Congress of the International Organization for Septuagint and Cognate Studies, Helsinki, 2010*, ed. Melvin K. H. Peters, SCS 59 (Atlanta: SBL, 2013), 397–411.

26 Aitken, "Language of the Septuagint," 134.

The Greek versions of books in this tradition often differ in noticeable ways from the Masoretic Text. These differences include, for example, nonstandard vocabulary choices, shifts in word order, and even entire sentences (or more) added, omitted, or relocated. In such cases, it is often difficult to know whether a translator was working from a Hebrew text like the Masoretic Text and going his own way, or whether he was translating mostly word for word but with a Hebrew text that differs significantly from anything we now know. These possibilities present scholars with numerous challenges that cannot detain us here (see the discussion in chap. 5). Suffice it to say that the details of books that fall into this translation tradition must be dealt with case by case.[27]

Even when we can say with confidence that a translator is consciously departing from his source text in translation, it is rarely easy to say why. Linguistic, cultural, and even theological considerations are often involved in ways that are not always possible (or desirable) to disentangle.[28] Of course, all those considerations influenced the Greek Pentateuch and the books in its tradition in certain ways too, as discussed above. Moreover, even the paraphrastic books contain sections in which the translation approach and linguistic style is extremely similar to the Pentateuchal tradition. So the difference between the Greek Pentateuch (along with the Pentateuchal tradi-

---

27 This issue is one of the classic conundrums of Septuagint textual criticism: to know whether a translator was departing from his source text in any given instance, one must first have a good sense for what the translator *usually* does in similar situations. But in order to know what a translator usually does, one must have a good sense for what source text he was working with.

28 It is also important to avoid imposing contemporary views of what constitutes a "good" or "accurate" translation on the ancient Jewish context, even in the descriptive terms we use to describe their practices, such as "literal" or "faithful" and so on, which can be unhelpfully (and unconsciously) value laden.

tion) and the paraphrastic tradition is more of a difference in degree than kind.[29]

The Revisional Tradition

A third tradition emerged not long after the paraphrastic tradition but with somewhat reversed tendencies. While the paraphrastic tradition was much *less* concerned with reproducing the wording of the Hebrew text (compared with the Pentateuchal tradition), the revisional tradition was much *more* concerned to do so. We have labeled this tradition revisional since it seems to have begun in the so-called Kaige movement in the first century BC, when existing translations were modified to more stringently follow the Hebrew text in Greek.[30] This process was undertaken in a number of books, such as Judges, Samuel–Kings, and the Minor Prophets. This same desire seems to underlie the later Jewish recensions, as discussed in chapter 4.

Yet it is important to understand that even as revisers took a more exacting approach to word order and lexical consistency in their work (a *translation* issue), they did not completely abandon matters of Greek convention and style (a *language* issue). They simply took a distinct approach. Ultimately, just as the translation and language of the Greek Pentateuch engendered a stylistic mindset for later Jewish writers in the Pentateuchal tradition, so too did the revisional tradition. Some

29 See Marieke Dhont, *Style and Context of Old Greek Job*, JSJSup 183 (Leiden: Brill, 2017).

30 Of course, the Hebrew text used during revision may not have been precisely the same as the one used for the original Greek translation itself. In fact, the major motivation for revisions was probably a preference for a translation of a slightly different Hebrew text or for a more exacting translation of the same Hebrew text, oftentimes closer to the (proto–)Masoretic Text in its wording.

books of the Hebrew Bible—such as Ecclesiastes, Lamentations, Song of Songs, and Ruth—were not revised with this mindset but were actually translated that way from the start.

Concluding Thoughts

We discussed in chapter 1 that it is incorrect and even misleading to think of the "Septuagint" as a unified entity, as if completed in full by a single translation committee. Now we have seen one major reason why. True, the Pentateuch was likely translated with some measure of coordination in third-century Egypt. Understanding the historical, social, and linguistic aspects of that context occupied our attention in the last chapter (and partly in this one), since it was in Egypt that diaspora Jews began to implement a stylistic model of translating Scripture that would greatly influence later work. But we have also seen how, soon after the production of the Greek Pentateuch, Jewish translation of Scripture diversified into a variety of approaches within three broad traditions, each with its own motivations and goals and all three existing concurrently over several centuries.

Recognizing this diversity should clarify why it is problematic to speak of "Septuagint translation technique" or "Septuagint Greek," as if—across the entire Greek Old Testament—there were only one thing to see. Nor is it accurate to dub the translation traditions discussed here as being either "dynamic" or "literal," since such simplistic labels fail to encapsulate all the complexities involved. These terms might say something minimal about how consistently word choice and word order are preserved in translation overall. But they convey nothing about matters of linguistic choice, such as style and register, which are inherent in all translation.

As we have looked at the various ways the Greek Old Testament was translated and how that work developed over time, we have also begun to see how earlier work influenced later work. Of course, for that to be possible, the physical, written texts of the Greek Old Testament had to be copied and distributed. The next chapter looks at that process in more detail.

4

How Did the Greek
Old Testament Develop?

WE HAVE NOW SEEN HOW the individual parts of the Greek Old Testament as a corpus appeared in different places, at different times, and with a variety of translation approaches and linguistic characteristics. All that activity occurred both *as* and *within* a broader, ongoing literary conversation in the context of the Jewish community in the ancient Mediterranean world.[1] Thus, it should come as no surprise that when it came to Scripture, the conversation involved both misunderstandings and disagreements as it progressed.

This chapter covers the nature of those misunderstandings and disagreements, as physical texts of the Greek Old Testament were used, copied, revised, and passed on through the decades and centuries up to the time of the early church. It is important to remember that this historical process involved Old Testament texts being

1 See Sean A. Adams, *Greek Genres and Jewish Authors: Negotiating Literary Culture in the Greco-Roman Era* (Waco, TX: Baylor University Press, 2020).

simultaneously copied and passed on in Greek *and* Hebrew, which influenced each other in certain ways. Although this chapter is primarily concerned with Greek, we must keep Hebrew in mind as well. In what follows, we will look at two key aspects of these historical developments:

1. Early revisions of Old Greek translations: How and why did the text of the original Greek translation of any given book of the Old Testament change over time?
2. Jewish and Christian recensions: How and why were new Greek translations of the Hebrew Bible made over time, and how did they influence later textual developments?

This chapter further demonstrates how misleading it is to speak of the "Septuagint" as if it were a singular entity. At the same time, the textual situation is not so complex that it should be regarded as hopelessly chaotic (even if it might feel that way at times!). While scholars are still debating many details—and while we wish more evidence were available—the Greek Old Testament does have a coherent and discernible history that is significant for the integrity and reliability of the text of Scripture as a whole.

Early Revisions of Old Greek Translations

Recall from our discussion in chapter 1 that the term Old Greek refers to the oldest, original translation of any given book of the Hebrew Bible. After it was produced, an Old Greek text was copied and distributed to a broader readership. At a general level, there are two ways an Old Greek text might change over time, one unintentional and one intentional.

Unintentional Textual Variants

The process of copying an entire book of the Bible by hand is extremely demanding work. It is understandable that sometimes mistakes occurred in the process. When scribes unintentionally copied something incorrectly as they worked, the result was a pair of manuscripts (the one used by the scribe and the resulting new copy) with disagreements between them. Those disagreements are known as *variants*.

There are many ways that variants were introduced in the copying process without any intention of doing so. For example, sometimes scribes inadvertently skipped over part of the text while looking back and forth between the original copy and the new copy. This mistake (known as parablepsis) often occurred when nearby words were the same (or had a similar beginning or ending), so that scribes may have *thought* they were continuing from where they had left off at last glance, but in fact they were not. Another kind of unintentional textual variant occurred when scribes simply misread specific words as they worked or perhaps misheard things if working with a colleague. For example, in Jonah 2:5 MT (2:4 ET), the Hebrew text reads, "look upon your holy *temple*" (Heb. *hechal*). The last word for "temple" was originally translated using *naon*, a suitable Greek equivalent. But at some point, a scribe mistakenly changed that word to *laon*, which means "people." That probably happened because the two words not only sound similar but also because they would have looked similar in the actual manuscripts (ΛΑΟΝ vs. ΝΑΟΝ).[2]

The upshot of this discussion is to recognize that in a world in which all written texts were made by hand, mistakes inevitably occurred,

---

2 Not only that, but the resulting phrase—"look upon your holy *people*"—still makes sense and echoes well-known phrases in Deuteronomy (7:6; 14:2). See further examples in Emanuel Tov, *The Text-Critical Use of the Septuagint in Biblical Research*, 3rd ed. (Winona Lake, IN: Eisenbrauns, 2015).

regardless of how meticulously the scribes worked. That is certainly not to say that no one cared about those changes. They did care, as attested by the many corrections and marginal notes in ancient manuscripts. Even so, as the Old Greek text was copied and recopied over the centuries, unintended (and often unnoticed) textual variants crept in. That said, it was not uncommon for changes to be made intentionally—and in some cases even extensively.

Intentional Textual Revisions

As already noted in chapter 2, in some cases it was not long after one person finished a Greek translation of a given book of the Hebrew Bible that someone else began to revise it. This activity indicates that disagreement arose within ancient Judaism over the nature of existing Old Greek translations in textual form or wording. Scholars agree that textual revision began to occur by the first century BC, if not earlier, but still debate its extent and rationale.

A major—although not exclusive—reason for this revision was the desire to bring existing Greek translations into closer alignment with the wording of the predominant (proto-Masoretic) Hebrew text. Nevertheless, parsing out precisely what motivated the revisers and just what kinds of changes they considered an "improvement" (and why) is rather challenging. As revisions piled on top of revisions, the textual history of some books in the Greek Old Testament became extremely complicated.

A useful way to understand the various approaches to and outcomes of textual revision is to consider the so-called "double text" books in the Greek Old Testament. For each of these books, the Old Greek text was revised to the point that its textual history split into two distinct traditions, as described in table 4.1.

Table 4.1   The Double Texts

Book	Tradition	Description
Esther	Old Greek	Closer to Masoretic Text but with many deviations and six additional chapters
	Alpha Text	Shorter version than Old Greek (~20%) but with same additional chapters
Daniel	Old Greek	Part of the paraphrastic translation tradition, with major additions
	Theodotion	Revised toward the Hebrew source text, with major additions
Judges	A text	Closer to the Old Greek translation in the Pentateuchal tradition
	B text	Revised toward the Hebrew source text with stylistic motivation

As convoluted as it may seem already, the textual history of each of these books is actually more complicated than table 4.1 indicates.[3] But these double texts help illustrate two major kinds of revisional changes in the course of the textual history of the Greek Old Testament. We will look at both kinds and then turn attention to the related matter of the Kaige movement.

CHANGES IN TEXTUAL SHAPE

Sometimes an existing translation was revised at a later point to significantly expand, abridge, or rearrange the text at the discourse level, usually with minimal or no reference to any source text (at least

3   Moreover, scholars past and present apply different labels to these textual traditions.

none known today). Esther provides a key example of the complexity. Although one tradition is labeled Old Greek, it is not certain whether it is actually the older tradition. The so-called Alpha Text is significantly shorter than both the Masoretic Text and the Old Greek text. But some scholars believe that the Alpha Text tradition of Esther was an independent translation (perhaps made from a Hebrew text no longer known) or even a kind of spin-off rewrite of the Esther story. Notably, both traditions of Greek Esther contain six chapters that are not present in the Masoretic Text. In this respect, Greek Esther shares something in common with Greek Daniel: both books contain lengthy additions that were originally written in Greek (rather than translated from a Hebrew source) and would eventually be considered part of the Apocrypha (see table 5.1 in chap. 5).[4]

CHANGES IN TEXTUAL WORDING

Of course, revision that changed the textual shape of a book at a literary level often involved or occurred alongside changes at a more detailed level. In most cases, these revisions adjusted textual wording in a way that more exactingly represented each word of a Hebrew source text and in the same order. This kind of activity should sound familiar from the last chapter, since these are the characteristics that would become typical of the revisional translation tradition.

Changes to textual wording occurred in different degrees and to different extents, depending on the profile of the book being revised. For example, the Old Greek versions of both Daniel and Judges were revised in their entirety, but the task looked quite

---

4   The additions to Greek Daniel are present in both textual traditions (though in different orders) and are known as Susanna, the Song of the Three Young Men, the Prayer of Azariah, and Bel and the Dragon.

different for each. The Old Greek translation of Daniel was part of the paraphrastic tradition, so its revision (largely preserved in Theodotion) required substantial reworking in word order and vocabulary choice. But the Old Greek translation of Judges (largely preserved in the A text) was more in line with the Pentateuchal tradition to begin with, so the revision (largely preserved in the B text) was not as thoroughgoing.

THE KAIGE MOVEMENT

The preceding discussion brings us to the murky waters of something known as Kaige.[5] Scholars vary widely in how they use this term: Is it a revision, recension, movement, or group? Generally speaking, it tends to serve as a catchall label for the Hebrew-oriented revisions to textual wording we have been discussing. Numerous characteristic features have been identified, though not all are equally useful. One notorious feature is the translation of the Hebrew particle *vegam* ("and also") with the Greek *kai ge* ("and also"), from which the term Kaige itself is derived.[6] The phenomenon was first noticed in portions of the text of Kingdoms (2 Sam. 11:2–1 Kings 2:11; 1 Kings 22–2 Kings 25), but the revisions to Greek Judges and Greek

5   The two groundbreaking studies on Kaige are Henry St. J. Thackeray, "The Greek Translators of the Four Books of Kings," *JTS* 8 (1907): 262–78; Dominique Barthélemy, *Les Devanciers d'Aquila*, VTSup 10 (Leiden: Brill, 1963). Barthélemy initially identified Kaige features in the Greek Minor Prophets Scroll (8ḤevXII gr) discovered in a cave near the Dead Sea in 1952. Earlier scholars refer to Kaige as "Kaige-Theodotion" or "proto-Theodotion," since the Kaige translation's features appear much later in the Theodotionic recension, discussed below.

6   Another common feature was the use of the Greek phrase *egō eimi* ("I am") to translate the Hebrew pronoun *'anoki* in distinction from the alternate form *'ani*, despite the syntactic oddities it produced. For others, see Tim McLay, "*Kaige* and Septuagint Research," *Text* 19 (1998): 127–39.

Daniel discussed above have also been associated with Kaige, as have the additions to Jeremiah.

Scholarship has advanced considerably on this topic in the last fifty years, but the issues involved remain complex and debates continue. One point of contention concerns which portions of what books can be labeled Kaige and how they fit into textual history. But the more foundational debates concern the criteria used to identify Kaige-style revision in the first place and how the tradition developed over time.[7] Recent research has pointed out how difficult it is to distinguish a revision (of a prior translation) from a new translation, especially if both resulting texts share a similar set of distinctive linguistic features that qualify as "Kaige" in some respect.

In addition, some of those linguistic features fit within Greek conventions, despite the fact that the Kaige tradition is usually characterized as "ultra-literal."[8] For example, the choice of the Greek *kai ge* to represent the Hebrew *vegam* coincides with increasing use of the particle *ge* in the first century BC in general, especially in more formal and literary writing. In that case, the choice to use it—whether in revision or new translation—was motivated not only by a desire to represent the Hebrew source text word for word but also by a desire to do so in an elevated

7   At one point, scholars had identified over ninety features that supposedly identified texts with Kaige-style revision, giving the impression that it was a coordinated and uniform effort (it was not). See further Robert A. Kraft, "Reassessing the Impact of Barthélemy's *Devanciers*, Forty Years Later," *BIOSCS* 37 (2004): 1–28; Leonard J. Greenspoon, "The *Kaige* Recension: The Life, Death, and Postmortem Existence of a Modern—and Ancient—Pheonomenon," in *XII Congress of the International Organization for Septuagint and Cognate Studies, Leiden, 2004*, ed. Melvin K. H. Peters, SCS 54 (Leiden: Brill, 2006), 5–16.

8   So Peter J. Gentry, "New Ultra-Literal Translation Techniques in Kaige-Theodotion and Aquila," in *Die Sprache der Septuaginta / The Language of the Septuagint*, ed. Eberhard Bons and Jan Joosten, LXX.H 3 (Gütersloh: Gütersloher Verlagshaus, 2016), 202–20.

register and with some stylistic effect.[9] It was that kind of approach to revision that seems to have inspired the later revisional tradition of translation itself in books like the Song of Songs. In this sense, the textual history of the Greek Old Testament and the various approaches to translation attested in the Greek Old Testament are intertwined.

Summary

As we have seen, unintentional variants affected the copying of the Greek Old Testament at every stage. More significant changes, however, were intentional and part of a revisional process that began early on. In some cases, revisions were made without reference to a source text, whether to expand, abridge, or rearrange. In other cases, a revision was made to adapt existing translations closer to the standard Hebrew text in circulation in first-century-BC Palestine (although not without subtle Greek stylistic concerns as well). That particular approach, often associated with the Kaige tradition, set the stage not only for later books translated in the revisional tradition from the start but also for even more rigorous new translations or recensions produced after the turn of the era.

Jewish and Christian Recensions

The textual history of the Greek Old Testament gets more complicated from here.[10] The trails multiply and begin to crisscross, while the footprints become harder to distinguish, whether they are too faint,

---

9 This phenomenon has been called "multicausality"; see James K. Aitken, "The Origins of KAI ΓE," in *Biblical Greek in Context: Essays in Honour of John A. L. Lee*, ed. James K. Aitken and Trevor V. Evans, BTS 22 (Leuven: Peeters, 2015), 21–40.

10 For further discussion of the issues involved, see Ville Mäkipelto, "The Septuagint and the Major Recensions," 161–74, and Peter J. Gentry, "The Septuagint and Origen's Hexapla," 191–206, both in *T&T Clark Handbook of Septuagint Research*, ed. William A. Ross and W. Edward Glenny (London: Bloomsbury T&T Clark, 2021).

too infrequent, or too similar to each other. The difficulty is largely due to the appearance of three new initiatives to translate the Hebrew Bible into Greek, known as "the Three" Jewish recensions.

The Three Jewish Recensions

AQUILA (α′)

Aquila lived in the second century AD during the reign of the Roman emperor Hadrian, who was in fact a close relative of his. Aquila joined the Christian community while living in Jerusalem but was ultimately excommunicated for continuing to practice astrology. He then converted to Judaism, studied under leading rabbis, and began his own Greek translation of the Hebrew Bible.

In the course of his work, Aquila did everything he could think of to represent every part of his Hebrew source text in Greek. To illustrate, Aquila went so far as to use the Greek preposition *syn* ("with") to represent the Hebrew direct object particle *'eth*, which does not actually need to be translated. The result of this approach would probably have been considered striking at best and confusing or even outrageous at worst.[11] Aquila's recension is marked by many other distinctive features, some of which intensified the approach that had begun with the Kaige movement. For example, Aquila wished to render the same Hebrew words by the same Greek words so scrupulously that he sometimes coined totally new Greek words to do it.

The cumulative effect of Aquila's translation approach was to use Greek in unusual, if not always totally unconventional, ways within his social context. That being said, it is worth noting that even *within* this

---

11 For example, in Gen. 1:1, Aquila's Greek translation effectively reads, "God created with [*syn*] the heavens and with [*syn*] the earth." In such situations, though, Aquila usually put the object of *syn* in the accusative case rather than the expected dative.

maximally stringent approach, Aquila nevertheless managed to interweave certain more educated and literary vocabulary and expressions in Greek. Overall, Aquila's work was well received among the Jewish community and remained popular for many centuries (particularly as Hebrew fell out of use).

SYMMACHUS (σ')

Aquila was not the only one producing a new translation of the Hebrew Bible. Although ancient writers attribute this second recension to someone named Symmachus, in reality we know almost nothing about who actually produced it. Most scholars believe the translator was a Jew living in Caesarea of Palestine, probably around the late second or early third century AD.

Although few scholars have investigated this recension in great depth, some consensus has emerged about the translation approach. It is useful to compare Symmachus with Aquila. On the one hand, the Aquila recension adopted and developed the tendencies of the revisional translation tradition and the Kaige movement. On the other hand, the Symmachus recension adopted and developed the tendencies of the Pentateuchal translation tradition. Symmachus is characterized by clarity of expression in Greek and accuracy in conveying the Hebrew, with stylistic choices familiar from the Greek Pentateuch. Yet in certain ways the translation choices in Symmachus move toward more conventional Greek. There are also theological elements in the recension that seem to be consistent with certain concerns in Jewish interpretation in Palestine, such as the tendency to translate the phrase "other gods" more specifically as "*false* gods" (e.g., Deut. 31:20).

In this sense, the two recensions—Aquila and Symmachus—extended earlier translation traditions, with some modifications, and yet were circulated and accepted within Jewish circles simultaneously. It seems that the Symmachus recension was aimed at a middle-class, native-Greek-speaking audience, one that was looking for Scripture in a different style and perhaps for different purposes than Aquila's version. Whatever demand existed for it initially, among both Jewish and Christian writers, it was Aquila's recension that ultimately became the primary Greek version within the late Roman and early Byzantine periods.

THEODOTION (θ′)

Yet another project was underway in the second century AD (perhaps even earlier) by someone named Theodotion. The identity of this historical figure is uncertain, but the most reliable source may be Irenaeus, who reports that Theodotion was a convert to Judaism originally from Ephesus.[12]

Many questions surround the nature of Theodotion's work. Epiphanius reports that Theodotion was translating from Hebrew but with some version of the Greek Old Testament close by.[13] Generally speaking, the approach was to produce a translation that is closer to the Hebrew than existing texts. The results were less rigorous than Aquila's work but not quite as stylish and idiomatic as Symmachus. Except for an inclination toward transcribing various terms, Theodotion's translation approach is otherwise fairly unremarkable, which makes it difficult for scholars to identify with certainty. For example, scholars disagree over whether so-called Daniel-Theodotion (see table 4.1) was truly produced by Theodotion and whether it was a new translation or simply a revision.

One major complicating factor amid the research on this recension is that Theodotion's translation approach has similarities with the

12 Irenaeus, *Haer.* 3.21.1.
13 Epiphanius, *De mens.* 17.

Kaige movement—or perhaps should be considered a later part of it. But the extent of those similarities is not consistent between books. As a result, scholars are uncertain whether Theodotion intentionally continued that translation tradition in his own work or simply produced his recension in consultation with a Greek Old Testament text that contained Kaige features without realizing it (or perhaps without caring). Whatever the case, the textual tradition that was later associated with or used by Theodotion was also familiar to some New Testament authors (e.g., Luke 21:27).

Origen's Hexapla and Its Recension

The appearance of the Three recensions is not the end of the story. In fact, these new texts prompted significant textual developments over the following centuries. A massive step in that development occurred in the third century at the hands of the Christian scholar Origen (ca. AD 185–254).

Given all the textual variation we have been discussing, it is tempting to conclude that the early church must not have cared much about the accuracy of the text of Scripture.[14] But that simply is not the case. The very existence of the revisions and recensions toward a standard Hebrew text demonstrates concern for textual accuracy among Jews going back at least into the first century BC, which in turn was carried further by Christians. Origen's work in the mid-third century AD was likely motivated by his concern with the state of the Old Testament

14 As suggested by Timothy M. Law, *When God Spoke Greek: The Septuagint and the Making of the Christian Bible* (Oxford: Oxford University Press, 2013), 139, 168. Although engaging and helpful in certain ways, Law's work is ideologically skewed, and his conclusions are often overstated. See Moisés Silva, review of *When God Spoke Greek: The Septuagint and the Making of the Christian Bible*, by Timothy Michael Law, *WTJ* 76, no. 1 (2014): 222–28.

text in his day and a desire to ensure that an accurate version was available for the church. In general, the amount of time, money, and effort expended among early Christians—Origen most of all—demonstrates the extremely high priority placed on the conformity of the text of the Greek Old Testament to the Hebrew Bible as the basis of the church's teaching and authority.[15]

Origen took unprecedented steps to remedy the situation as he saw it, setting out to provide an edition of the entire Old Testament in Greek that accurately conformed to the proto-Masoretic Hebrew text circulating in Palestine at that time. To do this, Origen launched a project known as the Hexapla ("sixfold"), in which he laid out the relevant texts in six columns on each page,[16] as shown in table 4.2. In each column of the Hexapla, Origen aligned the texts phrase by phrase for close comparison.[17]

Table 4.2   The Columns of the Hexapla

1	2	3	4	5	6
Origen's proto-Masoretic Hebrew text	Transcription of column 1 in Greek letters*	Aquila	Symmachus	Origen's Greek OT text**	Theodotion

*   Given that the full system of vowels had not yet been added to the Hebrew, column 2 supplied an oral reading tradition to help Origen (and others) pronounce column 1.

**   The text Origen chose for column 5 was not "the" Old Greek text or "the" Septuagint but one he felt was best or perhaps the one in widest distribution among Christians.

15   See further in chap. 7.
16   Jerome, *Comm. Tit.* 3.9.
17   Origen, *Comm. Matt.* 15.14; Eusebius, *Hist. eccl.* 6.16; Rufinus, *Hist.* 6.16.4.

It was a massive undertaking that probably filled around forty large volumes when completed.[18] But Origen was exceptionally well qualified for the job. Having lived in Alexandria until at least AD 220, Origen was educated in a tradition of extremely detailed textual and grammatical scholarship based in the royal library, which went back several generations to the time of Ptolemy I.

Although scholars still debate the details, recent research suggests that the Hexapla was a preparatory step for still more textual work, namely, a version known as the Tetrapla ("fourfold") that omitted columns 1 and 2. A major feature of the main Greek Old Testament text of the Tetrapla was the inclusion of changes that Origen made in consultation with the Hexapla. Origen marked all these changes using a set of symbols that the Greek scholar Aristarchus of Samothrace (ca. 217–145 BC) had perfected while editing Homer. The most common symbols included the following:

- The *obelus* (÷ or —) marked sections in the Greek Old Testament text that were not in the Hebrew text.
- The *asteriskos* (※) marked sections in the Greek Old Testament text not originally present but added from columns 3, 4, or 6 to match the Hebrew text.
- The *metobelus* (⸓ or ⸍) marked the end point of sections already marked with either an *obelus* or *asteriskos*.

Scholars do not agree on whether these symbols appeared in column 5 of the Hexapla itself or only in the Greek Old Testament text of the

18 See Anthony Grafton and Megan Williams, *Christianity and the Transformation of the Book: Origen, Eusebius, and the Library of Caesarea* (Cambridge, MA: Belknap Press of Harvard University Press, 2006), 96–132.

Tetrapla—or whether Origen actually created the Tetrapla first (if at all). Obviously, many areas of Hexapla research remain quite unsettled.

What is certain is that the edition of the Greek Old Testament text that was produced from Origen's fifth column, often called the "Hexaplaric recension," became extremely influential over the following centuries. Two later scholars—Pamphilus, the custodian of Origen's personal library, and Eusebius, bishop of Caesarea—continued to develop the text between AD 307 and 309, adding marginal notes and readings from the Hexapla. Before long, however, Origen's symbols were omitted from the text as it was copied. A major event in its distribution occurred when Constantine apparently ordered fifty copies from Eusebius for use throughout the empire, effectively making it the standard text.[19] Origen's work to reduce textual complexity thus led to an even more tangled legacy, one that scholars continue to labor mightily to undo.

The Antiochene Recension

There is yet another important Christian recension of the Greek Old Testament, which is perhaps the most controversial within Septuagint scholarship today. This recension is often known as the Antiochene or Lucianic text, since Jerome attributed it to the Christian martyr Lucian of Antioch (*Praef. ad Par.*). But the nature and extent of Lucian's involvement is unclear. Generally, Antiochene revisions are stylistic or clarifying in nature, occasionally introducing alternative readings from other Hebrew textual traditions. That being said, the characteristics of the Antiochene recension are not consistent across all books, making generalizations difficult.

19 Eusebius, *Vit. Const.* 4.36.

The most contentious issue related to this recension has to do with the base text that was used for the work. Scholars tend to speak of a proto-Lucianic text but differ over what relationship that earlier text has to other Greek Old Testament traditions, especially to texts within the Kaige movement. Some scholars argue that the proto-Lucianic text represented a revision of the entire Old Testament meant to align more closely with a *non*standard Hebrew text, given some similarities with texts found at Qumran (especially 4QSam^a). But this view has also been criticized for how little evidence supports it. Scholarly opinion on this topic is unsettled. Thankfully, important work is currently underway in Göttingen, Germany, where scholars are preparing critical editions of the books of Samuel and Kings in particular.

Summary

After the turn of the era, the text of the Greek Old Testament underwent significant and thorough changes. Chief among these are the Three, namely the Jewish recensions by Aquila, Symmachus, and Theodotion. While certainly informed by earlier Greek translations of the Hebrew Bible, their work represented new renderings in various styles yet largely within the existing translation traditions. Origen then used the Three, which he compiled in the Hexapla, to create an edition of the Greek Old Testament text that was closely aligned with the proto-Masoretic Hebrew text. While the Hexaplaric recension became extremely prevalent within Christendom, other Christian scholars like Lucian also worked at their own textual versions, although they are still not well understood.[20]

20 Jerome attests another Christian recension called the Hesychian recension (*Praef. ad Par.*), but we know virtually nothing about it.

Concluding Thoughts

At this point, it should be abundantly clear why speaking of the "Septuagint" as a singular, coherent textual entity is simply not possible. From the earliest translations of the Hebrew Bible through its scribal copying and early partial revisions to its later full recensions, the Greek Old Testament corpus is broad and multidimensional. This reality makes it difficult even to *find* the text of the "Septuagint," since there is still no single book that contains it (see the appendix for details).

We have seen how some books exist in different shapes and arrangements, while others attest linguistic styles that differ in both dramatic and subtle ways. A great deal of this activity occurred within Judaism itself as an outworking of different textual, cultural, religious, and linguistic preferences. Still other activity occurred within early Christianity as a response. To be sure, all the historical, linguistic, and textual cacophony underlying the "Septuagint" can be challenging to comprehend, but all of it has meaningful consequences for the study of the Bible and theology. It is to those concerns that we now turn our attention.

PART 2

———————

WHY DOES IT MATTER?

5

Why Does the Septuagint Matter
for Studying the Old Testament?

IN PART 1, WE ADDRESSED the first question posed in this book: What is the Septuagint? We now turn to the second question: Why does it matter?

In the next three chapters we will endeavor to show why knowledge of the Greek Old Testament is important for any student of the Bible—whether beginner or advanced—in terms of gaining a better grasp of the Old Testament (this chap.), understanding how the Greek Old Testament has shaped the New Testament (chap. 6), and probing the question of its authority in the church today (chap. 7). Each chapter covers much ground and delves into topics about which full books could be (and have been) written. As we cover the essentials, we will point out additional resources in the notes.

Though the significance of the Greek Old Testament for studying the Hebrew Bible may be obvious—insofar as it is a translation of it—such significance has often been overlooked or mishandled. Thus, in this chapter we will make the case for how the Greek Old Testament is essential for understanding three things:

1. The boundaries of the Old Testament: How has the Greek Old Testament influenced canon discussions, particularly with regard to the Apocrypha?

2. The contents of the Old Testament: What role does the Greek Old Testament play in reconstructing the wording of the Hebrew Bible?

3. Early interpretation of the Old Testament: How does the Greek Old Testament function as a kind of early Jewish "commentary" on the Hebrew Bible?

Taking each topic in turn, we will provide analogies or illustrative examples along the way to help clarify the main points.

The Boundaries of the Old Testament

As any fan of Middle Earth agrees, the core "canon" of J. R. R. Tolkien's *The Lord of the Rings* includes four books, from *The Hobbit* to *The Return of the King*. Additional books, however, such as *The Silmarillion* (including some of Tolkien's work as well as additions by his son Christopher Tolkien) and books that followed it, stand in a somewhat awkward relationship to the Tolkien "canon." If you packaged them all in a single box set with the original four, you might be signaling that they *all* are authentic canon. But considered individually, there would be much debate about where to draw the boundary around Tolkien's work. This is *roughly* the case when we consider the role of the Greek Old Testament in the reception of the Old Testament canon.

Judaism and all major branches of Christianity—Protestant, Roman Catholic, and Orthodox—acknowledge the same core set of Hebrew books as the nucleus of their canon of Israel's Scriptures:

the thirty-nine books (equivalent to the twenty-two by Jewish counting) from Genesis through Malachi, as known in the English order. In discussions of canon, the Greek Old Testament matters for this reason: *Roman Catholicism and the various branches of Orthodoxy accept both additional books and additional portions of canonical books owing in large part to their inclusion in the corpus of the Greek Old Testament.*[1] The Greek Old Testament, in other words, tends to blur the boundaries of the Old Testament to this day: that is, the existence of *Silmarillion*-like additions to an otherwise undisputed canonical core raises questions about what is "in" or "out" and why.[2] Thus, it is vital to shed some light on this complex topic.[3]

The Emergence of Jewish Greek Writings

Despite the importance of the Hebrew Bible, its books were not the only ones being written by the Jewish community over the centuries. Indeed, the Old Testament mentions other writings (now lost), such as the Book of Jashar (Josh. 10:12–13), the Book of the Wars of the Lord (Num. 21:14), the Book of the Acts of Solomon (1 Kings 11:41), and

---

1   Space does not permit us to explore the Old Testament canons of the Ethiopian, Coptic, and Syrian churches.

2   A related issue is the sequencing of the Old Testament books. The notion that the English Bible follows "the Septuagint" sequence instead of "the Hebrew" is an oversimplification: the sequence in the Hebrew Bible was not standardized until the rabbinic period (ca. AD mid-100s–600s), and the complete Greek Old Testament manuscripts do not all agree on the sequence—nor do they match the English sequence.

3   See Greg Lanier, *A Christian's Pocket Guide to How We Got the Bible: Old and New Testament Canon and Text* (Fearn, Ross-shire, Scotland: Christian Focus, 2019); Lee M. McDonald, *The Formation of the Biblical Canon*, vol. 1, *The Old Testament: Its Authority and Canonicity* (London: T&T Clark, 2017).

others. Jewish literary productivity picked up, however, after 400 BC, as briefly introduced in chapter 2.

Numerous "intertestamental" Jewish writings are collectively known as the Dead Sea Scrolls (and related literature). They were composed mostly in Hebrew between the third century BC and first century AD, and they range from apocalyptic visions of battles between light and darkness to poetry that evokes the biblical psalms.[4] Another set of Jewish writings is loosely grouped under the title Pseudepigrapha, spanning several languages (Hebrew, Aramaic, Ethiopic, Syriac, Coptic, Latin, Greek) and periods (some are pre-Christian/Jewish, some are post-Christian, and some are a blend). They include a host of writings such as 1 Enoch (quoted in Jude 14–15), Jubilees, 4 Ezra, 2 Baruch, the Sibylline Oracles, and the Testaments of the Twelve Patriarchs.[5]

Most important for our purposes are the so-called books of the Apocrypha (which means "hidden"). They emerged around the last three centuries BC and have reached us primarily in Greek, either as new compositions or as translations from Hebrew.[6] They represent a variety of Jewish viewpoints, span several genres, and include additional books as well as additional *portions* of biblical books (see table 5.1).

Though they differ at the margins, Roman Catholicism and the Orthodox churches broadly ascribe scriptural authority to these books,

---

4 Michael Wise, Martin Abegg Jr., and Edward Cook, eds., *The Dead Sea Scrolls: A New Translation* (New York: HarperOne, 2005).

5 James H. Charlesworth, ed., *The Old Testament Pseudepigrapha*, 2 vols. (Peabody, MA: Hendrickson, 2010).

6 David A. deSilva, *Introducing the Apocrypha: Message, Context, and Significance*, 2nd ed. (Grand Rapids, MI: Baker Academic, 2018). It is widely agreed that at least 1 Maccabees, Sirach, and Tobit were originally composed in Hebrew or Aramaic.

Table 5.1   Greek Apocrypha

Additional Books	Additions to Canonical Books
1 Esdras (occasionally 2 Esdras)	Esther: ~6 chapters
Tobit	Psalms: Ps. 151
Judith	Jeremiah: Epistle of Jeremiah, Baruch
Wisdom of Solomon	
Sirach (or Ecclesiasticus)	Daniel: Susanna, Song of the Three Young Men, Prayer of Azariah, Bel and the Dragon
Prayer of Manasseh	
1 Maccabees	
2 Maccabees	
3 Maccabees	
4 Maccabees	

denoting them *deuterocanonical* ("second canon").[7] Given that they have circulated mostly in Greek, how did the Greek Old Testament itself influence this development?

The Role of the Greek Old Testament

The influence of the Greek Old Testament on the trajectory of the Greek Apocrypha can be traced in two ways: the usage of the writings and their inclusion in Old Testament codices.

USAGE

Though composed within Jewish communities, Apocryphal books met with mixed reception within Judaism in subsequent decades.

---

7   They agree on 1–2 Maccabees, Tobit, Judith, Sirach, Wisdom of Solomon, and the additions to Esther, Jeremiah, and Daniel. Beyond this, Orthodox churches typically add 1 Esdras, 3 Maccabees, Prayer of Manasseh, and Psalm 151 (with 4 Maccabees included in an appendix). The treatment of 2 Esdras varies considerably over time.

Some were read or quoted by the Qumran community,[8] but Philo largely ignored them, Josephus made only selective use of them, and major Greek recensions (Aquila, Symmachus, and Theodotion; see chap. 4) skipped them.

Within Greek-speaking Christianity, however, the story was different. As early as the late 200s and early 300s, these Apocryphal books had obtained broad circulation among the churches, as shown by patristic quotations and their varied inclusion in early Old Testament canon lists.[9] The question of their status came to a head with Origen (ca. AD 185–253), Jerome (ca. AD 345–420), and Augustine (AD 354–430). Origen and Augustine, though disagreeing on some details, were persuaded that Apocryphal books should be sanctioned as authoritative within the church because they had attained widespread reception:[10] If the Greek-speaking church was already using a Greek Old Testament that included additional writings not found in Hebrew, why stop them?

Jerome, however, took a different position. He affirmed the value of the Apocrypha for personal devotional "edification," but he argued that only the accepted Hebrew books (i.e., Genesis–Malachi) should be used for deciding matters of ecclesiastical "dogma."[11] Yet he did translate some of the Greek Apocryphal books for his Latin Vulgate. Ironically, in due course his distinction between the

8 Sirach, Tobit, the Epistle of Jeremiah, and a variant form of Psalm 151 were found among the Dead Sea Scrolls.

9 See Edmon L. Gallagher and John D. Meade, *The Biblical Canon Lists from Early Christianity: Texts and Analysis* (Oxford: Oxford University Press, 2018).

10 Origen, *Ep. Afr.* 4–5, 13; Augustine, *Doctr. chr.* 2.8; *Civ.* 17.20; 18.36.

11 Jerome, *Praef. ad Sal.*; preface to the Vulgate. For a fuller treatment of the Augustine-Jerome debates, see Annemaré Kotzé, "Augustine, Jerome and the Septuagint," in *Septuagint and Reception: Essays Prepared for the Association for the Study of the Septuagint in South Africa*, ed. Johann Cook, VTSup 127 (Leiden: Brill, 2009), 245–62.

traditional Old Testament books (for dogma) and the Apocrypha (for edification) would prevail among Protestants (though they otherwise moved away from the Vulgate). But Jerome's distinction would be undone by his Roman Catholic successors, who granted certain Apocryphal writings (mediated via the Vulgate) equal canonical status at the Council of Trent (1546). Thus, both directly through the debates on church usage and indirectly through Jerome, the Septuagint—or, more precisely, the corpus of Jewish religious writings in Greek—shoulders much responsibility for how the boundaries of the Old Testament within today's Roman Catholic Church encompass certain Apocryphal books.

CODICES

The broad use of Apocryphal books is also reflected in their inclusion in certain manuscripts of the Greek Old Testament. For much of antiquity, biblical books (or groups of books) were copied on separate scrolls. But with the progress of book-binding technology came the possibility of including the entire Old Testament (and eventually New Testament) between two covers—permitting collections of writings in the form of a codex (much like the Tolkien "box set" analogy). Importantly, all the larger codices of the Greek Old Testament, dating from the fourth century AD and beyond (and all produced by Christians) include not only the traditional Old Testament books but also subsets of the Apocrypha (see table 5.2).[12]

---

12 Some earlier manuscripts of sections of the Old Testament also include Apocryphal additions (e.g., Susanna in Papyrus 967).

Table 5.2   Apocryphal Books Found in Major Greek Codices

	Sinaiticus	Vaticanus	Alexandrinus
1 Esdras		✓	✓
Tobit	✓	✓	✓
Judith	✓	✓	✓
Wisdom of Solomon	✓	✓	✓
Sirach	✓	✓	✓
Prayer of Manasseh			✓
1 Maccabees	✓		✓
2 Maccabees			✓
3 Maccabees			✓
4 Maccabees	✓		✓
Additions to Esther	✓	✓	✓
Additions to Psalms (Ps. 151)	✓	✓	✓
Additions to Jeremiah		✓	✓
Additions to Daniel		✓	✓

None of the major codices fully agree on the Apocrypha included between their covers (or their ordering). Nevertheless, because of the Greek Orthodox Church's reception of the Greek Old Testament as its authoritative text, these codices played a significant role in its adoption of the Apocrypha.[13]

Summary

Which canon, then, is right? The traditional Hebrew one (adopted by Jews and Protestants) or the expanded "Septuagintal" canon that

13 See the introduction to *The Orthodox Study Bible* (Nashville: Thomas Nelson, 2008); Alexandru Mihăilă, "The Septuagint and the Masoretic Text in the Orthodox Church(es)," *RESt* 10, no. 1 (2018): 30–60.

includes various Apocryphal writings (adopted, though with differences, by the Roman Catholic and Orthodox Churches)? We probe this important question in chapter 7. For now, we simply want to underscore that the Greek Old Testament matters because of the role it has played on this front. The Apocryphal books were composed or translated into Greek by Jews in tandem with the efforts to translate the traditional Hebrew books. They were in turn used and passed on within the Greek-speaking early church and beyond until the label "Septuagint" was applied in a catchall way to the whole (varied) collection in much of Christendom. Without this phenomenon, the boundaries of the Old Testament would likely be the same among all branches of Christianity.

The Contents of the Old Testament

Let us shift to how the Greek Old Testament affects the study and reconstruction of the Hebrew text of the Old Testament, focusing on the undisputed books (i.e., Genesis–Malachi).

Recent years have seen the rise of the "director's cut": revisions to an already-released movie that involve removing scenes, adding scenes, overlaying commentary, and so forth. The movie remains recognizable relative to its authentic original but has been meaningfully revised.

Something like this can be said for the Old Testament books, in which the Greek Old Testament sometimes plays a kind of "director's cut" role. As described in chapter 1, the main form of the Hebrew Bible today is the Masoretic Text, chiefly presented in the medieval Leningrad Codex. Its contents, however, go back much earlier, and the manuscripts of the Greek Old Testament are a critical link in that chain. They provide much earlier access to the Hebrew text as it stood more than a millennium before the Masoretic Text. The Greek Old Testament matters, then, for this reason (building on chaps. 3–4): *while on the whole the Greek translations of canonical books are more or less the same as the traditional Hebrew, the* shape *or specific* wording *varies relative to the Hebrew in a significant number of places.*

For instance, if you turn to the story of David and Goliath (1 Sam. 16–18) in Greek, you will find quite a different retelling than that found in the Masoretic Text (and thus in English translations). And a quick glance at the Old Testament footnotes of, say, the ESV or NIV reveals numerous wording variations, many of which reference the "Septuagint." Let us explore such phenomena.

The Shape of the Biblical Books

By *shape* (or *text form*) we mean the macroliterary features of the book, such as the number and sequence of chapters, plot episodes, narrative or poetic structure, and so forth—akin to a "director's cut" edition that provides an alternate ending or cuts entire scenes. Contrary to some scholars who give the impression that biblical books in the Greek Old Testament are virtually unrecognizable relative to their Hebrew counterparts (particularly the Masoretic Text),[14] the overall shape of most books is identical. You know you are reading Genesis—the Greek translation is not about alien space invaders or the Arabian nights, any more than a director's cut is an entirely different movie. That said, there are some important differences (introduced in prior chapters) that should be noted by students of the Old Testament.[15]

---

14 Particularly Timothy M. Law, *When God Spoke Greek: The Septuagint and the Making of the Christian Bible* (Oxford: Oxford University Press, 2013), 74–79.

15 Emanuel Tov, "The Nature of the Large-Scale Differences between the LXX and MT S T V, Compared with Similar Evidence in Other Sources," in *The Earliest Text of*

LARGER EXAMPLES

The six best known examples involve substantial differences in length, ordering of material, or both.

- Exodus 35–40: The tabernacle account in Greek is substantially shorter and arranged differently than the Masoretic Text.[16]
- 1 Samuel 16–18: The account of David and Goliath in Greek is condensed compared to the Masoretic Text, particularly excluding large sections of chapters 17 and 18.[17] As a result, the flow and details of the plot are discernibly different.
- Jeremiah (excluding Apocryphal additions): The Greek is about one-eighth shorter than the Masoretic Text, and its chapters are arranged differently after chapter 25.[18] For instance, the famous chapter 31 (on the "new covenant") is actually chapter 38 in the Greek, and the "Righteous Branch" passage found in chapter 33 is absent altogether in the Greek. Importantly, Hebrew fragments of Jeremiah found at Qumran (4QJer[b,d]) appear to reflect something like this shorter, rearranged Greek version.
- Ezekiel: The Greek form is around 5 percent shorter than the Masoretic Text and includes a variety of other rearrangements (e.g.,

---

the Hebrew Bible: The Relationship between the Masoretic Text and the Hebrew Base of the Septuagint Reconsidered, ed. Adrian Schenker, SCS 52 (Atlanta: SBL, 2003), 121–44; Eugene Ulrich, "The Old Testament Text and Its Transmission," in *The New Cambridge History of the Bible*, vol. 1, *From the Beginnings to 600*, ed. James Carleton Paget and Joachim Schaper (Cambridge: Cambridge University Press, 2013), 92.

16 The narrative is ~4,800 words in English (ESV; ~4,000 in Hebrew) but only ~3,200 in Greek. This difference was observed as early as Origen, *Ep. Afr.* 5.

17 The narrative is ~3,100 words in English (ESV; ~2,500 in Hebrew) but only ~1,800 in Greek.

18 See the versification table in Andrew G. Shead, "Jeremiah," in *T&T Clark Companion to the Septuagint*, ed. James K. Aitken (London: T&T Clark, 2015), 418.

Ezek. 7:1–11) or shortenings (e.g., Ezek. 36:23–28). Moreover, the Greek form found in Papyrus 967 reorders chapters 36–39.

- Job: The Greek form is around one-sixth shorter than the Masoretic Text, though it also includes several added passages (e.g., a longer speech by Job's wife at Job 2:9). And various lines of the characters' speeches are regularly skipped, modified, or rearranged.
- Proverbs: The Greek form differs from the Masoretic Text in both additions and omissions of several verses throughout but also in macro rearrangement, particularly the relocation of material in chapters 30–31.

SMALLER EXAMPLES

A handful of other Greek passages differ from their Hebrew counterparts in ways that stretch beyond ordinary textual variation (covered in the next subsection), though not quite to the degree as those listed above. Select examples include the following:

- Joshua 24: The Greek includes additional material that elevates the status of Joshua.
- 1 Samuel 2: Hannah's song differs in content and order in all three known forms: Greek, Qumran (4QSam), and Masoretic Text.
- 1 Kings 20–21: The order of these chapters is switched in the Greek form.
- Nehemiah 11: The Greek form lacks several verses found in Hebrew.
- Psalms: Numbering differs by roughly one between Psalms 10 and 147 owing to splitting or combining of various psalms; for instance, Psalm 119 in Hebrew is Psalm 118 in Greek.[19] (This is

---

19 For details, consult Karen H. Jobes and Moisés Silva, *Invitation to the Septuagint*, 2nd ed. (Grand Rapids, MI: Baker Academic, 2015), 376–80.

typically denoted by placing the Greek chapter number in square brackets; e.g., Ps. 119[118]).

There is no one-size-fits-all explanation for these fascinating phenomena, but two hypotheses receive the most attention.

On the one hand, in some cases the Greek translator may have had access to a Hebrew form that circulated outside the mainstream of tradition that culminated in the Masoretic Text. This is an attractive possibility for, say, Jeremiah; the book itself admits that the prophet created two copies, one of which was longer (Jer. 36:32). Perhaps the shorter one circulated in Egypt (where Jeremiah spent time) and was used for the Greek translation, while the longer one may have circulated in Babylon or Palestine after the exile and was used by the Masoretes.[20]

On the other hand, some of the divergences in shape or text form might be best explained as more aggressive, intentional reworkings of the Hebrew text by translators (recall chap. 4). This appears to be the case for Job, where the Greek translator may have deliberately condensed or rearranged speeches to reduce what seemed repetitious or redundant.[21] It may also be a possibility for Exodus 35–40, if the translator was seeking to smooth out the repetitions of tabernacle instructions earlier in Exodus.

Consensus explanations have yet to be reached on these differences in shape or text form. Though they are few enough in number

---

20 Suggested in Peter J. Gentry, "The Text of the Old Testament," *JETS* 52, no. 1 (2009): 19–45.

21 Suggested by Gentry, "Text," 28; Law, *When God Spoke Greek*, 55. Some scholars, however, defend the hypothesis that Greek Job was using a different Hebrew text than what is preserved in the Masoretic Text.

so as not to distort the overall picture of stable literary development and translation processes, such phenomena should cause any serious student of the Old Testament to pause and reflect—to which we return in chapter 7. If nothing else, these Greek "director's cut" variations of biblical books show the Greek Old Testament to be an interesting object of study in its own right, not only as a point of comparison to the Hebrew tradition. The shorter forms of, say, Jeremiah or the narrative of David and Goliath provide intriguing insight into the use and reuse of Old Testament writings over a long period of time.

The Text or Wording of the Biblical Books

Moving from the forest to the trees, the Greek Old Testament also plays a major role in understanding the text or wording of the biblical books at a detailed level. In this case we are referring not to the larger-scale differences in the literary shape of a book (covered above) but to the differences we find between clauses or words in the Hebrew tradition and their counterparts in Greek—as when a "director's cut" overdubs a word in the original.[22]

Numerous times wording found in the Greek Old Testament, if retroverted into Hebrew, varies from that found in the Masoretic tradition (or any other known Hebrew witnesses). The Greek might read ABCD and the Masoretic Text ABBD. Most of these differences arise for reasons already discussed related to translation or textual history and give us no reason to doubt the Hebrew text. But in many cases it appears that the Greek wording may have a superior claim to

22 Note that we are not concerned in this section with the textual variants in the scribal tradition of the *Greek Old Testament* itself (for which, see chap. 4); rather, we are concerned with comparing the reconstructed Old Greek text with the *Hebrew*.

authenticity than the wording found in the traditional Hebrew text; for instance, the Greek variant ABCD is probably better than the ABBD reading in the Masoretic Text and could be used to emend it.[23] In such situations the Greek Old Testament, particularly the reconstructed Old Greek, is like finding lost archival footage of a movie, giving access to the earlier and superior reading that has apparently changed over time. And a Greek variant's claim to originality is strengthened when it is corroborated by the same wording elsewhere (i.e., Dead Sea Scrolls, Latin Vulgate, Syriac Peshitta, Aramaic Targums).

Debates over instances where the Old Greek may be better than the known Hebrew abound in the scholarly literature. A quick way to get a feel for these variations is to sample where even a textually conservative translation like the ESV adopts wording *from the Greek Old Testament* (which it labels "Septuagint") as the main text, placing the Masoretic Hebrew wording in the footnotes (see table 5.3). The ESV's footnotes also acknowledge wording variants in the Septuagint that "shed possible light on the text" but do not override the Hebrew (e.g., Gen. 4:8; 1 Sam. 13:1; numerous others).[24]

None of this is new news, as most English translations do a generally good job of making the data available when they use the Greek Old Testament text-critically. Nevertheless, students of the Bible need to know that the Greek Old Testament plays a major role in restoring the Hebrew text where our traditional manuscripts in the Masoretic tradition are less than pristine.

---

23 See Emanuel Tov, *The Text-Critical Use of the Septuagint in Biblical Research*, 3rd ed. (Winona Lake, IN: Eisenbrauns, 2015); Anneli Aejmelaeus, "What Can We Know about the Hebrew *Vorlage* of the Septuagint?" *ZAW* 99, no. 1 (1987): 58–89.

24 Quoted from the ESV preface (2011 edition).

Table 5.3   Examples of the ESV Adopting "Septuagint" Wording

Verse	Hebrew Wording (ESV Footnote)	"Septuagint" Wording (ESV Main Text)
Gen. 47:21	he removed them to the cities	he made servants of them
Ex. 1:22	—	to the Hebrews
Ex. 8:23	set redemption	put a division
Ex. 20:18	the people saw	the people were afraid
Deut. 32:8	sons of Israel	sons of God
Deut. 32:43a	Rejoice his people, O nations; —	Rejoice with him, O heavens; bow down to him, all gods*
Deut. 32:43b	—	He repays those who hate him
Judg. 14:15	seventh day	fourth day
Judg. 18:30	Manasseh	Moses
1 Sam. 10:1	Has not the LORD anointed you to be prince over his heritage.	Has not the LORD anointed you to be prince over his people Israel? And you shall reign over the people of the LORD and you will save them from the hand of their surrounding enemies. And this shall be the sign to you that the LORD has anointed you to be prince over his heritage.

Table 5.3 (*continued*)

Verse	Hebrew Wording (ESV Footnote)	"Septuagint" Wording (ESV Main Text)
1 Sam. 14:41	Therefore Saul said to the LORD, the God of Israel,	Therefore Saul said, "O LORD God of Israel, why have you not answered your servant this day? If this guilt is in me or in Jonathan my son, O LORD, God of Israel, give Urim. But if this guilt is in your people
	"Give Thummim."	Israel, give Thummim."
Isa. 51:19	how shall I comfort you?	who will comfort you?
Ezek. 18:17	from the poor	from iniquity
Zech. 5:6	eye	iniquity

* These lines are also found in 4Q44 of the Dead Sea Scrolls.

Summary

Some scholars have surveyed all these observations and concluded that "the biblical text was characterized by variety" and that the data "undermine the impression of stability gained from reading modern Bibles."[25] Such views are undoubtedly overstated. The six major differences in literary shape listed above come from portions of the Old Testament that make up less than five percent of the whole.[26] And while

---

25 Law, *When God Spoke Greek*, 44–45; similarly, Møgens Müller, *The First Bible of the Church: A Plea for the Septuagint*, JSOTSup 206 (Sheffield: Sheffield Academic Press, 1996), 100–104.

26 We calculated this percentage by summing the Hebrew words of the areas in question (e.g., the three chapters of 1 Samuel) and dividing by the total Hebrew word count in the Old Testament.

wording variations are numerous, the number of times the Old Greek is deemed superior to the Hebrew is judged relatively small even by most critical scholars. The overall shape and specific wording of the Old Testament books attested in both Hebrew and Greek traditions are remarkably consistent and stable.

Nevertheless, a student, pastor, or layperson could benefit from paying attention to the Greek Old Testament when preparing a Bible lesson. Textual deviations, whether large or small, may be relevant for the key step of confirming the text one believes should be taught or preached. Indeed, the fact that most English translations are *already* doing this means their footnotes cannot be ignored altogether. Those involved in educating laity not only need to have a better handle on what is going on under the hood of the Old Testament but also need to be able to explain things clearly to inquiring Bible readers who, too, notice "Septuagint" in their Bible's textual footnotes.

Early Interpretation of the Old Testament

As covered in chapter 3, the translation of a writing from one language to another is a complex affair that extends well beyond a mechanical one-to-one mapping of the words of the source to the words of the target language. (This is why computerized translations so often disappoint.) Before one can make a competent translation, the source text must be *understood.* That is, the translator's task always involves some measure of interpretation.

This is certainly true for the Greek Old Testament, which confers on it another layer of significance for today: *the Greek translations provide an early interpretation of the Hebrew Bible, helping us understand Jewish theology at a particularly important time of its development.* This kind of "commentary" is a valuable window into the Jewish world that is a primary backdrop of the New Testament era.[27]

Insight into Difficult Hebrew

Numerous passages present modern readers with challenges in discerning the meaning of the Hebrew.[28] In such cases, the Greek translations can at least provide perspective on how *some* Jewish readers understood difficult passages in their day. A few illustrative examples may help.

GENESIS 1:2

The precise meaning of the Hebrew adjectives describing primordial creation in Genesis 1:2—*tohu* and *bohu* ("without form and void," ESV)—is debated. The Old Greek translator gives his own take by rendering them "invisible and uncompleted," using the negating *alpha* for both (Gk. *aoratos* and *akataskeuastos*) to describe what creation was *not*—which the next creative acts of God remedy.[29]

EXODUS 34:29–30

When Moses descends Mount Sinai after conversing with God, a rare Hebrew verb (*qaran*) derived from "horn" is used to describe his face's luminescence in Exodus 34:29–30. Confusion about this word led some Renaissance artists to depict actual horns coming from Moses's

---

27 On the Greek Old Testament as "commentary," see Martin Hengel, *The Septuagint as Christian Scripture: Its Prehistory and the Problem of Its Canon*, OTS (Edinburgh: T&T Clark, 2002), xi; Sidney Jellicoe, *The Septuagint and Modern Study* (Oxford: Clarendon, 1968), 316.

28 The note that "the meaning of the Hebrew is uncertain" is not infrequent in, say, the ESV (e.g., Isa. 10:27; 27:8; Jer. 5:26; 8:7, 13, 18; 15:11).

29 Colossians 1:16 uses *aoratos* in the same way.

head. The Old Greek translator, however, is much closer to the mark, using the word "glorify" to describe what happens to Moses.[30]

ISAIAH 42:1

Scholars have long followed in the footsteps of the Ethiopian eunuch (Acts 8:34) in inquiring about the identity of the "servant" in Isaiah's famous servant songs. The Hebrew tradition of Isaiah 42:1 leaves the question unanswered, simply referring to "my servant" and "my chosen." The Old Greek translator, however, adds "Jacob" to the former and "Israel" to the latter, clearly taking this song to refer to God's corporate people.

HOSEA 6:7

The Hebrew word in the clause "*ke'adam* they transgressed the covenant" in Hosea 6:7 has long been debated: does it refer to Adam's transgression of the covenant of works in Genesis 2 or simply to humanity's ongoing transgressions? Nearly all modern English translations read, "like Adam" (e.g., ASV, CSB, ESV, NASB, NIV, RSV), while the KJV reads, "like men." The Old Greek translator clearly holds the latter view with "like man" (*hōs anthrōpos*).[31] Even if a modern reader disagrees with a Greek translator's take on a Hebrew passage, the information is still useful for providing insight into Jewish interpretation centuries before our day.

Contemporary Application

As introduced in chapter 3, one interesting feature of the Greek Old Testament is an occasional tendency to update the wording of the

---

30 This rendering in turn affected Paul's discussion of this scene in 2 Cor. 3:7–15.
31 When the Greek translators refer to the person "Adam" elsewhere, the transliteration is typically used (Gk. *adam*).

Hebrew text to adapt it to the present-day situations of the translators, effectively "actualizing the prophecies for the community of [their] own time."[32] In addition to the examples covered before, we could mention a few others that give a sense of this practice.[33] In Exodus 1:11, the translator adds "which is Heliopolis" to clarify the current name of a city; in Deuteronomy 23:18, the translator adds "no sorceresses" and "no initiates" to the command not to take prostitutes, likely to address Egyptian mystery cults of that period; in Joshua 10:2, the Greek term "metropolis" is used to translate the Hebrew "royal city"; and in Isaiah 9:11 and 66:19, the terms "Greeks" and "Greece" are used, respectively, to identify foreign enemies (instead of "Philistines") and territories.

These examples are not, in themselves, exegetically significant, nor do they have much text-critical weight; rather, they are akin to explaining "Babylon" today as "modern-day Iraq." Yet they do reveal how Jewish translators desired to elucidate and apply the Hebrew in a way that their contemporary readers would understand—a conviction shared not only today but also in the New Testament period.

Theological Exegesis

Of greater importance are the ways in which the translators reveal their theology through translations that deviate intentionally, albeit sometimes subtly, from the Hebrew wording.[34] Though the Greek translators

32 Abi T. Ngunga and Joachim Schaper, "Isaiah," in Aitken, *T&T Clark Companion to the Septuagint*, 406.

33 See Martin Rösel, "Translators as Interpreters: Scriptural Interpretation in the Septuagint," in *A Companion to Biblical Interpretation in Early Judaism*, ed. Matthias Henze (Grand Rapids, MI: Eerdmans, 2012), 64–91.

34 Studying such deviations requires that we reconstruct the earliest, most authentic Hebrew and demonstrate that the Greek translation has deviated intentionally. Many potential examples of theological exegesis are thus disputed because of the complexity of such analysis; the ones provided here, however, are widely agreed on. The very idea

generally translate their source conservatively (see chap. 3), there are certainly some cracks where their views of God shine through.

DIVINE METAPHORS

The Hebrew Bible often uses rich metaphors to describe the unseen God of Israel, often depicting him using human attributes (e.g., "hands," "feet") or objects in the physical world (e.g., "tower," "shield"). The Greek translators appear to downplay such language. Scholars debate exactly why, but for the translators located in Egypt, at least, their goal may have been to dissociate the true God from the Egyptian pantheon and its ties to birds, cattle, sun, moon, and so forth. The most prominent example is the almost uniform way that the dozens of Hebrew "God is my rock" metaphors are translated without using "rock" (Gk. *petra*) in the Greek translation. Sometimes the translators simply use "God" (Gk. *theos*) in place of "rock" (e.g., Deut. 32:18; Ps. 18[17]:32; Isa. 30:29), but sometimes they use a different word like "helper" or "protector" (e.g., Pss. 18[17]:3; 89[88]:27; Isa. 26:4).[35]

DIVINE NAMES

The translation of the Hebrew names of God also proves intriguing. The most famous is "I AM WHO I AM" at Exodus 3:14, where there remains much debate on how precisely to take the Hebrew. The Old Greek translation is "I am the one who is" (*egō eimi ho ōn*). This is not only a compelling translation of the Hebrew, but it reflects the Jewish

---

of a "theology" of the Septuagint remains debated; see Hans Ausloos and Bénédicte Lemmelijn, "Theology or Not? That's the Question: Is There Such a Thing as 'the Theology of the Septuagint'?," in *The Theology of the Septuagint*, ed. Hans Ausloos and Bénédicte Lemmelijn, LXX.H 5 (Gütersloh: Gütersloher Verlagshaus, 2020), 19–45.

35 Staffan Olofsson, *God Is My Rock: A Study of Translation Technique and Theological Exegesis in the Septuagint*, ConBOT 31 (Stockholm: Almqvist & Wiksell, 1990).

concept that Israel's God is the self-existent source of all existence. He is simply "the being One." Other translations of divine names are worth mentioning. The Hebrew "LORD of hosts" (*tseva'oth*)—possibly referring to angelic armies—is typically translated "Lord All-Mighty" (Gk. *pantokratōr*), conveying the total sovereignty of Israel's God. And "Most High" (Heb. *'elyon*) is typically translated with *hypsistos*, a Greek term often used for pagan deities like Zeus, possibly signaling a kind of subtle polemic against false gods.

CLARIFICATIONS

Some verses reveal how the translators apparently attempt to correct perceived theological issues in the Hebrew source text (the need for this and their success in doing so are beside the point).[36] For instance, the Greek of Genesis 2:2 makes an interesting modification to the creation account. The Hebrew reads that God "finished his work on the *seventh* day" and then rested. The Old Greek reads that he "finished his work on the *sixth* day" and then rested. It seems that the translator is trying to mitigate any possible misunderstanding that God *worked* on the seventh day, so he changes it to the sixth.[37] Another example is Exodus 15:3, where the Old Greek translator takes the Hebrew "the LORD is a man of war" and renders it "the Lord is one who breaks wars," possibly out of a desire to make God less violent.[38] The Old Greek translator also shows monotheistic sensitivity in Numbers 25:2, where the plural

---

36 On such theological "clarifications," see Martin Rösel, "Towards a 'Theology of the Septuagint,'" in *Septuagint Research: Issues and Challenges in the Study of the Greek Jewish Scriptures*, ed. Wolfgang Kraus and R. Glenn Wooden, SCS 53 (Atlanta: SBL, 2006), 239–52.

37 Jellicoe, *Septuagint*, 321–22; Mark W. Scarlata, "Genesis," in Aitken, *T&T Clark Companion to the Septuagint*, 19.

38 Rösel, "Translators as Interpreters," 86–87.

"gods" (Heb. *'elohim*) is rendered with "idols" (Gk. *eidōloi*), denigrating their status and clearing up any possible misconceptions (since the same Hebrew word can be used for Israel's God). Finally, the translators also show a striking consistency in rendering the Hebrew word "altar" (*mizbeakh*) with two different words in Greek—*thysiastērion* for the true altar of God and *bōmos* for false altars of pagan deities—to prevent any confusion about which "altar" is which.

These examples need not be considered "correct" translations, but they certainly shed light on the theology of the translators, who, at times, could not help but bring it to the table when unpacking the meaning of the Old Testament and capturing it in Greek.

Messianic Exegesis

Finally, while most studies of the development of Jewish messianic ideas prior to the Christian era have focused on the Dead Sea Scrolls, Pseudepigrapha, and Apocrypha,[39] the Greek Old Testament also deserves attention. On occasion the Greek translators subtly transform their Hebrew source in ways that give a glimpse of messianic ideology.[40]

GENESIS 49:10

In Jacob's blessing on Judah in Genesis 49:10, the Hebrew reads,

> The scepter shall not depart from Judah,
>   nor the ruler's staff from between his feet. (ESV)

---

39 The scholarly literature is too vast to summarize here; see Gregory R. Lanier, *Corpus Christologicum: Texts and Translations for the Study of Jewish Messianism and Early Christology* (Peabody, MA: Hendrickson, 2021).

40 Michael A. Knibb, ed., *The Septuagint and Messianism*, BETL 195 (Leuven: Peeters, 2006); Johan Lust, *Messianism and the Septuagint: Collected Essays*, BETL 178 (Leuven: Peeters, 2004).

The Greek translator personifies the metaphor, substituting "ruler" (Gk. *archōn*) for "scepter" and "leader" (Gk. *hēgoumenos*) for "ruler's staff." This likely sets the stage for numerous other Jewish writings that interpret the prophecy messianically.[41]

NUMBERS 24:7, 17

A similar modification appears in the Old Greek of Balaam's famous "star" oracle. In place of the difficult Hebrew of Numbers 24:7, "Water shall flow from his buckets," the Greek translator substitutes "A man [Gk. *anthrōpos*] will come forth from his offspring." Later, in Numbers 24:17, where the Hebrew speaks of a "scepter" arising from Israel (as in Gen. 49:10), the translator reads, "man," once more. This passage proves influential in Jewish messianic development,[42] and the Greek introduction of an eschatological "man" is a key part of that picture.

ISAIAH 28:16

The "stone" passage in Isaiah 28:16 becomes quite important in the New Testament (with Ps. 118[117]:22 and Isa. 8:14), but its messianic trajectory likely begins with the Greek translator. After promising a "stone" in Zion, the Hebrew reads, "Whoever believes will not be in haste" (ESV). The Old Greek, however, adds the object of faith: "Whoever believes *in him*." This personifies the stone as an object of

---

41 E.g., 4Q252; 1 Macc. 3:1–9; Philo, *Mos.* 1.289–91; Targum Onqelos (at this passage); several rabbinic writings.

42 Helen R. Jacobus, "Balaam's 'Star Oracle' (Num 24:15–19) in the Dead Sea Scrolls and Bar Kokhba," in *The Star of Bethlehem and the Magi: Interdisciplinary Perspectives from Experts on the Ancient Near East, the Greco-Roman World, and Modern Astronomy*, ed. Peter Barthel and George H. van Kooten, TBN 19 (Leiden: Brill, 2015), 399–429.

faith, which—combined with the eschatological importance of Zion in the Old Testament—suggests that the translator understands the "stone" as a messianic metaphor.[43]

TRACES OF PREEXISTENCE

While the Hebrew Bible is somewhat reticent on the preexistence of a messianic deliverer, at least two Old Greek glosses may suggest that the idea was developing within Judaism. First, Psalm 72[71]:1 praises the king, and then verse 17 in Hebrew states,

> May his name endure forever,
>> his fame continue as long as the sun. (ESV)

The Greek, however, renders the second clause "May his name endure *prior to* the sun," using the Greek *pro* likely in a temporal way. A similar feature is found in Psalm 110[109]:3, where the Hebrew speaks of the king in cryptic terms:

> From the womb of the morning,
>> the dew of your youth will be yours. (ESV)

The Greek, however, reads, "From the womb, before the morning-star, I have begotten you," which again may suggest precreational existence.[44]

---

43 Jaap Dekker, *Zion's Rock-Solid Foundations: An Exegetical Study of the Zion Text in Isaiah 28:16*, OtSt 79 (Leiden: Brill, 2007).

44 For more on messianism in the Greek Psalms, see Joachim Schaper, *Eschatology in the Greek Psalter*, WUNT, 2nd ser., vol. 76 (Tübingen: Mohr Siebeck, 1995). Cf. Mic. 5:2[1], where the shepherd-king from Bethlehem is described in the Greek thus: "His goings-out are from the beginning, from the days of eternity."

DANIEL 7:13

The heavenly vision of "one like a son of man" in Daniel 7:13–14 is a tremendously important Old Testament passage. Space does not permit engaging in the debates on "son of man" in Judaism and the Gospels. Of most interest here is the (Aramaic) clause "He came *to* the Ancient of Days" (ESV). While other Greek translations have this figure come "unto" or "before" (*heōs*) the Ancient of Days, the Old Greek reads, "He came *as* [*hōs*] the Ancient of Days."[45] Whether this is simply a scribal error remains debated, but such an interpretation that essentially fuses the identity of the "son of man" with the "Ancient of Days" may have influenced both Jewish messianism and the New Testament.[46]

Other so-called messianizations within the Greek Old Testament could be mentioned (e.g., "he" [Gk. *autos*] at Gen. 3:15), but these suffice to demonstrate the point: some translational decisions in the Greek Old Testament—alongside other writings like the Dead Sea Scrolls—may contribute to our understanding of messianic ideas leading up to the New Testament era.

Summary

We have covered several areas in which the Greek Old Testament provides an angle on how some early Jewish communities interpreted the

---

45 This reading is presented in the Rahlfs-Hanhart edition and is found in all Old Greek manuscripts (notably Papyrus 967), though the Göttingen edition emends it to *heōs* ("unto").

46 Such influence might be reflected in the heavenly, preexistent "son of man" in 1 Enoch 48.2–3 and 4 Ezra 13.25–26, as well as in the way Rev. 1:13–14 applies the attributes of the "Ancient of Days" to "one like a son of man." See R. Timothy McLay, *The Use of the Septuagint in New Testament Research* (Grand Rapids, MI: Eerdmans, 2003), 155–59.

Bible: grappling with difficult Hebrew, applying the ancient text in a way that speaks to a contemporary audience, and inserting theological and messianic ideas as they developed within Judaism. For this reason, students of the Bible would benefit from approaching the Greek Old Testament as an early Jewish commentary on Scripture, aiding our understanding of the Old Testament as well as the Jewish world in which it was passed on to the early church.

Concluding Thoughts

In this chapter we have noted three key areas in which a more-than-cursory knowledge of the "Septuagint" matters for Old Testament studies.

In much the same way that publications such as *The Silmarillion* are treated as Tolkien canon by some readers of *The Lord of the Rings*, additional Greek books (such as 1 Maccabees) and additional portions of books (such as Susanna, added to Daniel) are received as canonical by the Roman Catholic and Orthodox Churches largely because of their relationship to the Greek corpus of Jewish religious texts. Thus, any student interested in why the boundaries of the Old Testament differ within Christendom must know something about the Greek tradition.

We have also covered how the Greek translations of the canonical Hebrew books function, at times, as a kind of "director's cut," as with the two forms of Jeremiah. Such differences need not imply that the Greek should replace the Hebrew, only that in the centuries after the authoring of such books and prior to the stabilization of the Masoretic Text, there were alternative text forms in use. But there are nevertheless times when the Greek translations—being more ancient than the primary Masoretic Text manuscript used today—*do* provide access to a better form of the text at the clause or word level. Thus, the study of the Greek Old Testament is valuable for understanding, and at times reconstructing, the wording of the Hebrew Bible.

Finally, because of the dynamics of translation, students of the Greek Old Testament can gain insight into Jewish interpretive principles, theology, and messianism by studying the Greek translations, particularly where they deviate from the known Hebrew.

But it matters not only for the Old Testament. If the Greek translations circulated in forms that sometimes deviate from the known Hebrew, and if some of those deviations are a window into Jewish religious beliefs in the pre–New Testament period, then the Greek Old Testament likely has tremendous significance for the study of the New Testament as well. We turn to this topic in chapter 6.

6

Why Does the Septuagint Matter for Studying the New Testament?

THOUGH THE GREEK TRANSLATIONS of the Hebrew Bible are significant from the perspective of the study of the Old Testament, they are also extremely relevant from the other direction: the study of the New Testament. In fact, many people first catch a whiff of this thing called the "Septuagint" through their study of the New Testament and, in particular, its quotations of the Old Testament. For such students of the Bible, the mysterious "Septuagint" becomes a kind of portal to a whole new world.[1]

The aim in this chapter is to map some of the terrain of this world. We will examine how the Greek Old Testament is essential for understanding three things:

---

1 Martin Hengel notes, "The New Testament exegete . . . dealing for the first time more thoroughly with the problem of the LXX as a whole, quickly observes how very much he has entered a *terra incognita*, full of surprises." *The Septuagint as Christian Scripture: Its Prehistory and the Problem of Its Canon*, OTS (Edinburgh: T&T Clark, 2002), 19.

1. The "Bible" of early Christianity: In what sense is it proper to call the Greek Old Testament the "pew Bible" of the New Testament writers and early church?

2. The language of the New Testament: How did the Greek translations of the Old Testament shape the style and vocabulary of the New Testament writers?

3. The use of the Greek Old Testament in the New Testament: How do New Testament authors interact with the Greek Old Testament text when quoting Scripture?

In other words, we will explore how the Greek Old Testament attained prominence in the New Testament era, followed by two ways it influenced the New Testament. By probing these questions, this chapter will help today's readers of the Bible have a clearer picture of how and why the Greek Old Testament matters for studying the New Testament itself.

The "Bible" of Early Christianity

One question a visitor to a church often asks is "What Bible do they use?" A church's Bible says a lot about it. But it can be a complex question to answer. Though occasionally quoting from other versions in a sermon, a pastor typically preaches from one specific Bible version, which in turn is likely the church's pew Bible. Yet individual congregants may use other versions—even other languages—or they may access the Bible in a variety of ways (apps, verse-a-day emails, devotional books, audio Bibles, braille readers, memory, and more). On any given Sunday, the NIV may be in the pulpit, a Spanish Bible on someone's tablet, and a tattered KJV on the back row. Pinning down the day-to-day Bible of a modern church is a complex task.

The situation is similar when we turn to the ancient church. In seeking to understand early Christianity, the Greek translations of the Old Testament matter immensely: *this corpus is in some sense the dominant "pew Bible"*[2] *of the New Testament authors and early church—though we must also appreciate the complexity of the situation.* In fleshing this out, we want to guard against a common misconception, voiced here: "The LXX was the Bible of the authors of the New Testament. . . . The LXX was transmitted in Christian circles once it was adopted as the official Bible of the Church."[3] We examine the kernel of truth underlying this notion but also show how the diverse means by which early Christians accessed the Old Testament prevent us from overstating how the "Septuagint" is *the* "official Bible" of the New Testament church.

Greek Speakers and a Greek "Bible"

The data suggest that early Christians, including the authors of the New Testament, indeed made extensive use of the Greek translations of the Old Testament as part of the broader shift toward the language.

As discussed in chapter 2, large portions of the Jewish community adopted postclassical Greek in the 300s BC and thereafter. The extent to which Greek penetrated the Jewish world, both outside and within Palestine, is shown by the use of Greek for the Old Testament

---

2 In this section, "Bible" refers primarily to the Old Testament. We place it in quotation marks when the singular use of the word would be anachronistic for the first century.

3 Natalio Fernández Marcos, *The Septuagint in Context: Introduction to the Greek Version of the Bible*, trans. Wilfred G. E. Watson, 2nd ed. (Leiden: Brill, 2000), 338. Similarly, Martin Hengel writes, "The use of the LXX as Holy Scripture is practically as old as the church itself." *Septuagint*, 22. And Møgens Müller remarks, "The Church . . . supported the Greek translation of the OT books as a true expression of its Bible." *The First Bible of the Church: A Plea for the Septuagint*, JSOTSup 206 (Sheffield: Sheffield Academic Press, 1996), 143.

translations themselves, other Jewish literature (e.g., Philo, Josephus, some of the Pseudepigrapha), inscriptions, papyri (e.g., business receipts, letters), and personal names.[4]

It is unsurprising, then, that the early movement of Jesus's followers, being birthed out of Judaism, was just as open to using Greek. Jewish-background Christians such as Paul were thoroughly conversant in Greek despite knowing at least Hebrew (Acts 21:40; 22:2). The use of dual names—one Semitic, one Greek—is well-attested in the apostolic circle,[5] and two apostles had Greek names (Philip and Andrew). Even in Jesus's day, people were coming to hear him from Greek areas like the Decapolis (Matt. 4:25; cf. John 12:20), so Greek was necessary at some level to communicate. Though some Jewish-background churches continued leaning toward Aramaic or Hebrew, the rapid inclusion of Gentile-background Christians caused Greek-speaking churches to crop up quite early (Acts 6), led by Greek converts like Stephen and Apollos. And the abiding reminder of the language preference of the apostolic movement is the writing of the New Testament in Greek. It was a Greek world under Caesar, so most early Christians used Greek.

Therefore, in much the same way that a pastor of a Korean-speaking church quotes from a Korean Bible rather than, say, a Portuguese one in a Sunday sermon, it is only natural that the Greek-speaking Christians—both Jewish-background and Gentile—would default to a Greek "Bible."

We see this first with the apostolic authors. The New Testament does not explicitly mention which version of Scripture they use, but

---

4 Martin Hengel, *Judaism and Hellenism: Studies of Their Encounter in Palestine during the Early Hellenistic Period*, trans. John Bowden, 2 vols. (Philadelphia: Fortress, 1974).

5 For example, Saul/Paul, Levi/Matthew, Simon/Peter, Judas/Thaddaeus, John/Mark, Joseph/Justus.

their quotation patterns provide insight. Given that the New Testament is written in Greek, obviously all Old Testament quotations are too. But the more significant and less obvious point is this: a large number of Old Testament quotations in the New Testament follow verbatim (or nearly so) the wording found in the majority Old Greek translation.[6] This includes both situations in which there is no real difference between the known Hebrew and Old Greek forms of a passage and situations in which they differ and the New Testament author follows the latter (to which we return below). In either case, the close correspondence in wording shows that the source from which the New Testament authors often draw is the Greek Old Testament. Indeed, some like Luke and the author of Hebrews make near *exclusive* use of the Greek Old Testament. It would make strategic sense, when the apostles proclaim Christ as the fulfillment of the Old Testament, to use a Greek form already widely available to their audiences.[7]

The seven New Testament quotations of Leviticus 19:18 illustrate the point (Matt. 19:19; 22:39; Mark 12:31; Luke 10:27; Rom. 13:9; Gal. 5:14; James 2:8). Five authors quote Leviticus 19:18, yet each quotation shares identical wording, and that wording matches the Old Greek *exactly*. None of the writers—even in Gospel narratives, where the speakers may have quoted Leviticus in a Semitic form—offer an independent translation of the Hebrew or an alternative Greek rendering. Rather, they all quote precisely the same Old Greek text.

---

6 For attempts at quantifying the percentage of agreement of New Testament quotations with Old Testament sources (Hebrew, Septuagint, etc.), see Gleason Archer and Gregory Chirichigno, *Old Testament Quotations in the New Testament* (Chicago: Moody Press, 1983), xxv–xxxii; Fernández Marcos, *Septuagint in Context*, 324.

7 Archer and Chirichigno, *Old Testament Quotations*, ix.

We also see an extensive use of the Greek Old Testament in the postapostolic period among the Greek-speaking church fathers. As the church spreads away from its Jewish roots, working knowledge of Hebrew becomes the exception (e.g., Origen, Jerome), not the rule, leaving Greek as the only real option for accessing the Old Testament for much of the church. Fathers such as Justin, Clement of Alexandria, and Irenaeus frequently use the Greek Old Testament, particularly the Old Greek text they often call the "Septuagint."[8]

As a result, there is some truth to the notion that the Greek translations of the Old Testament—often the text now known as the Old Greek—functioned as the "pew Bible" of many Greek-speaking Christians, from New Testament authors to key church fathers.

Appreciating the Complexity

While the early church made frequent use of the Old Greek, there was never a council that "adopted" the "Septuagint" as "official." Thus, equating it with *the* "Bible" of the New Testament era can be misleading. Let us examine why.

OTHER AVAILABLE "BIBLES"

For Jesus and the apostolic circle, the Hebrew Bible, in whatever form(s) it took, was still around despite the overarching shift to the Greek language. Jesus most likely reads from a Hebrew scroll of Isaiah in Nazareth (Luke 4:17–20).[9] Matthew employs Hebrew directly in his "Immanuel"

---

8   See Edmon L. Gallagher, "The Septuagint in Patristic Sources," in *T&T Clark Handbook of Septuagint Research*, ed. William A. Ross and W. Edward Glenny (London: Bloomsbury T&T Clark, 2021), 255–67.

9   It is likely that Hebrew scrolls were still in use in Palestine at this time. S. Safrai, "The Synagogue," in *The Jewish People of the First Century: Historical Geography,*

and "My God, my God" quotations (Matt. 1:23; 27:46). Some bilingual Jewish authors of the New Testament appear to draw on a Hebrew text in certain quotations[10]—indeed, some scholars have suggested that certain quotations in the New Testament are closest to the Hebrew wording found in the Dead Sea Scrolls.[11] And Revelation may have been "influenced most by the Hebrew rather than the Greek Old Testament."[12]

Additionally, the apostles could have had access to portions of the Old Testament in Aramaic form,[13] which may have been circulating orally or in written form by the first century.[14] A variety of studies have attempted to trace the possible influence of the Old Testament in Aramaic on early Christians.[15]

Finally, the New Testament authors occasionally show familiarity with recensions of the Greek Old Testament. For instance, Matthew 26:64 describes the "Son of Man" coming "on [Gk. *epi*] the clouds," reflecting the Old Greek of Daniel 7:13—while Luke 21:27 reads, "in [Gk. *en*] the clouds," reflecting the tradition of Theodotion. And

---

Political History, Social, Cultural and Religious Life and Institutions, CRINT 1.2, ed. S. Safrai and M. Stern (Philadelphia: Fortress, 1976), 2:908–44.

10 E.g., Matt. 2:15, 18; 4:15–16; John 19:37; Rom. 11:35; 1 Cor. 2:9; 3:19; 14:21; 15:54; 2 Cor. 8:15; 2 Tim. 2:19.

11 J. de Waard, *A Comparative Study of the Old Testament in the Dead Sea Scrolls and in the New Testament*, STDJ 4 (Leiden: Brill: 1966).

12 G. K. Beale, *John's Use of the Old Testament in Revelation*, JSNTSup 166 (Sheffield: Sheffield Academic Press, 1999), 62.

13 Aramaic words are found in, e.g., Matt. 5:22; Mark 5:41; 7:34; 14:36; John 20:16; Rom. 8:15; Gal. 4:6; 1 Cor. 16:22.

14 Though the major Aramaic Targums were not finalized until post–New Testament times, the discovery of Aramaic Job (11Q10) among the Dead Sea Scrolls indicates the existence of some written Aramaic translations.

15 E.g., Mirsław Wróbel, "The Gospel according to St. John in the Light of Targum Neofiti I to the Book of Genesis," *BPT* 9, no. 4 (2016): 115–30; Adam Howell, "Finding Christ in the Old Testament through the Aramaic Memra, Shekinah, and Yeqara of the Targums" (PhD diss., Southern Baptist Theological Seminary, 2015).

some of Paul's quotations, when deviating from the Old Greek, may be drawing not on the Hebrew itself but on a Greek text (now lost) that was already revised toward the Hebrew.[16]

In the patristic era, we see similar patterns. Some fathers occasionally consult later Greek recensions (Aquila, Symmachus, Theodotion).[17] The Old Latin was popular in the Western church in the second century.[18] And the Old Syriac translation was widely used in the third- and fourth-century Syrian church. It is thus an oversimplification to say that the "Septuagint" alone was the "official Bible of the Church."[19]

DIFFERENT WAYS OF ACCESSING THE "BIBLE"

Moreover, much like today's era of print, smartphones, tablets, and audiobooks, in antiquity there were multiple ways of accessing the Old Testament. Oral transmission was alive and well, such as liturgical readings in the synagogue (Acts 15:21). Many Jewish-background Christians likely had extensive portions of the Old Testament memorized as well.[20] Early Christians may have accessed small collections of favored Old

16 Dietrich-Alex Koch, "The Quotations of Isaiah 8,14 and 28,16 in Romans 9,33 and 1 Peter 2,6.8 as Test Case for Old Testament Quotations in the New Testament," *ZNW* 101, no. 2 (2010): 223–40; Ross Wagner, *Heralds of the Good News: Isaiah and Paul "in Concert" in the Letter to the Romans*, NovTSup 101 (Leiden: Brill, 2000), 126–31.

17 Reinhart Ceulemans, "Greek Christian Access to 'the Three,' 250–600 CE," in *Greek Scripture and the Rabbis*, ed. Timothy M. Law and Alison Salvesen, CBET 66 (Leuven: Peeters, 2012), 165–91.

18 This was not a singular or complete translation, but it is important for textual scholarship because the translation preceded the major recensions. See Julio Trebolle Barrera, "Vetus Latina," in *Textual History of the Bible*, ed. Armin Lange and Emanuel Tov (Leiden: Brill, 2016), 1:319–30.

19 Fernández Marcos, *Septuagint in Context*, 338.

20 Andrew Montanaro, "The Use of Memory in the Old Testament Quotations in John's Gospel," *NovT* 59, no. 2 (2017): 147–70; Wagner, *Heralds*, 20–28; Birger Gerhardsson, *Memory and Manuscript: Oral Tradition and Written Transmission in Rabbinic Judaism and Early Christianity*, ASNU 22 (Uppsala: Almqvist, 1961).

Testament excerpts to avoid lugging around scrolls when traveling.[21] Finally, apostolic authors could access the Old Testament through written copies in various synagogues or copying centers,[22] and in the tumultuous first century, there was no guarantee that such Old Testament copies in Rome, Corinth, Ephesus, or Jerusalem would be identical (cf. multiple editions of the NIV: 1978, 1984, 1996 [NIrV], 1999, 2002 [TNIV], 2011).

Two examples may help illustrate the complexity of pinning down the "pew Bible" of the early church. The first is the case of the New Testament quotations of the sixth, seventh, and eighth commandments (murder, adultery, and theft). Their order in the Old Greek texts of Exodus 20 and Deuteronomy 5 differ from each other *and* from the Masoretic Hebrew.[23] Such differences could explain why the multiple quotations in the New Testament (Matt. 19:18; Mark 10:19; Luke 18:20; Rom. 13:9; James 2:11) differ from each other too, with some following the Hebrew order and some the Old Greek of Deuteronomy. Yet the forms of the commands differ also: Matthew and Paul adopt the Old Greek's negated future, while Mark, Luke, and James use a negated subjunctive, perhaps from a different Greek text or oral tradition.[24]

A second illustration is the use of Isaiah 6:9–10 five times in the New Testament (Matt. 13:14–15; Mark 4:12; Luke 8:10; John 12:39–40; Acts

21 For a detailed study of such testimonia, see Martin C. Albl, *"And Scripture Cannot Be Broken": The Form and Function of the Early Christian Testimonia Collections*, NovTSup 96 (Leiden: Brill, 1999). The discovery of collected excerpts in Judea (4Q174, 4Q175) and Egypt (P.Oxy. 4933) lend credence to this hypothesis, though it remains debated.

22 Christopher D. Stanley, *Paul and the Language of Scripture: Citation Technique in the Pauline Epistles and Contemporary Literature*, SNTSMS 74 (Cambridge: Cambridge University Press, 1992), 78.

23 The Nash Papyrus (150–100 BC) also differs from the Masoretic Text.

24 See Gregory R. Lanier, "Scriptural Inspiration and the Authorial 'Original' Amid Textual Complexity: The Sequences of the Murder–Adultery–Steal Commands as a Case Study," *JETS* 61, no. 1 (2018): 47–81.

28:25–27). Each quotation differs from the others (and from known Hebrew and Greek Old Testament forms) in terms of clause order and wording (though the wording in Matthew and Acts are closest to each other), and such deviations could have arisen from liturgical use, memory, or oral tradition.

Both examples illustrate how the New Testament authors were not all carrying around an identical, leather-bound *Septuagint: First-Century Edition* as their only "Bible." Sometimes, at least, they appear to have made use of various available options and means of accessing them—not unlike today, if one pastor quotes the NIV 1984 from memory and another consults the NIV 2011 in print.

Summary

What is the upshot of this discussion? While there is much truth to the claim, it is too simplistic to say that the "Bible" of early Christianity was *the* "Septuagint." Though there was no carbon-copied "Septuagint" in the back of every pew in the early church, the corpus of Greek translations of the Old Testament still likely predominated. The Greek Old Testament is thus rightly considered the most influential middleman or bridge between the Hebrew text of ancient Israel and the increasingly Greek-speaking early church.[25]

If this is true, how did such influence play out? We next look at its influence on the *language* of the New Testament, followed by its influence through *quotations* of the Old Testament in the New Testament.

---

25 Karen Jobes writes that the Greek Old Testament "forms a bridge that mediates the literary and theological concepts between the Hebrew Bible and the Greek NT." "When God Spoke Greek: The Place of the Greek Bible in Evangelical Scholarship," *BBR* 16, no. 2 (2006): 221.

The Language of the New Testament

For centuries one particular version of the Bible has played the dominant role in the English world: the King James Version. From its
"thee" and "thou" to its poetic cadence and its specific phrasing for
passages such as the Lord's Prayer, the KJV stands unrivaled in how
it has shaped the religious language of English-speaking Christians.

The same is more or less true for the Greek Old Testament. As, in
some limited sense, the "pew Bible" of the New Testament writers,
the Greek Old Testament matters because *it inevitably shaped their
language, particularly in terms of style and vocabulary.*[26] This is not to
say that there is a special kind of "Holy Spirit Greek" or even "Jewish
Greek." But just like you might slip into "thine is the kingdom" even
if you never say "thine" otherwise, the peculiarities of the Greek Old
Testament left its mark on those who used it.[27]

Style

As surveyed in chapter 3, often the Greek translators attempt to reflect
the grammatical features of their Hebrew source (e.g., word order)
with varying results as Greek. In much the same way as "Yoda speak"
(from Star Wars) is still English, just rearranged, the end result in the
Greek Old Testament is occasionally something that is still intelligible
as Greek but reads more like Hebrew.

---

26 Here we distinguish *style* (surface-level choices of phrasing) from *syntax* (the grammatical nuts and bolts of the language). Current research generally limits the influence of the Greek Old Testament on the New Testament to the former.

27 Jennifer M. Dines observes, "The LXX exercises a profound influence on vocabulary and style, though this varies from writer to writer and is not all-pervasive."
The Septuagint, UBW (London: T&T Clark, 2004), 143. See also Karen H. Jobes
and Moisés Silva, *Invitation to the Septuagint*, 2nd ed. (Grand Rapids, MI: Baker
Academic, 2015), 200–205.

Such Hebrew-like features in the Greek Old Testament sometimes bleed through in the New Testament,[28] whether intentionally or unintentionally—even when no direct Old Testament quotations are in play. A few examples include the following:[29]

- "He [or she] answered and said"—mainly in narratives (e.g., Luke 13:15)
- Frequent use of parataxis: "and . . . and . . . and" (e.g., Matt. 4:24–25)
- "And it happened that" (Gk. *kai egeneto*) to begin a narrative (e.g., Mark 1:9)
- *En tō* + infinitive for concurrent action ("while") (e.g., 1 Cor. 11:21)
- "He [or she] opened the mouth and said" (e.g., Matt. 5:2)
- "He added to [Gk. *prostithēmi*] and did X" for "continued to do X" (e.g., Acts 12:3)
- Use of *megas* ("great") redundantly, as in "they rejoiced with great rejoicing" (e.g., Matt. 2:10)

The infancy narrative of Luke 1–2 offers a comprehensive example of this phenomenon. Though Luke is capable of writing formal Greek (Luke 1:1–4), the phrasing, sentence structure, poetry, and even overarching narrative flow of these chapters seem like what one would find in the Greek of Genesis or 1 Samuel (denoted 1 Kingdoms in the Greek Old Testament). In other words, they ring more Hebraic than Greek.

28 We leave aside the debates about whether or when to call these "Semiticisms/Hebraisms" or "Septuagintalisms."

29 See further in Ralph Brucker, "Die Sprache der Septuaginta und das Neue Testament: Stil," in *Die Sprache der Septuaginta / The Language of the Septuagint*, ed. Eberhard Bons and Jan Joosten, LXX.H 3 (Gütersloh: Gütersloher Verlagshaus, 2016), 460–72.

Most of these patterns are not themselves "un-Greek," but their concentrated presence in the New Testament shows that the Greek Old Testament was so familiar that it often shaped the apostolic writers' stylistic choices, making it rather important for today's students who want to understand the Greek of the New Testament better.

Vocabulary

The Greek Old Testament also influences the New Testament's use of specific vocabulary. The decisions made by the Greek translators to render certain Hebrew words with certain Greek words gained momentum, sometimes giving the latter a particular slant in meaning. Such words are not special—they are still words, at the end of the day—but they can carry a more technical sense in a Jewish-Christian context. This is similar to how *skin of my teeth* makes little sense unless you know the KJV or how *devotional* has a specific meaning in the church that differs from the meaning used outside it.

Given the New Testament authors' broad exposure to the Greek Old Testament, it is not surprising that they would often employ the narrower ranges of meaning for some words, making the Greek Old Testament a kind of "urban dictionary" for the New Testament. Several prominent examples might be mentioned (see table 6.1).[30] In addition to these examples, the Greek Old Testament paves the way for many Semitic loanwords or transcriptions commonly found in the New Testament, such as *hallēlouia* ("Hallelujah"), *amēn* ("amen"), *manna* ("manna"), and *pascha* ("Passover").

---

30 See detailed discussions in R. Timothy McLay, *The Use of the Septuagint in New Testament Research* (Grand Rapids, MI: Eerdmans, 2003), 146–48; Emanuel Tov, "Three Dimensions of LXX Words," *RB* 83, no. 4 (1976): 529–44.

Table 6.1   Greek Old Testament Influence on New Testament Vocabulary

Word	Typical Secular Greek Use	Narrowing in the Greek OT	Influence on NT	Example
akrobystia	(none)	newly coined term for "foreskin"	used for "uncircumcised" instead of *akroposthia*	Rom. 2:25
christos	"to be rubbed on"	"anointed [one]," for Heb. *mashiakh*	honorific for Jesus "Christ" ("Messiah")	numerous
diathēkē	"last will" (cf. *synthēkē*, "contract")	divine "covenant," for Heb. *berith*	divine covenants	Luke 22:20
doxa	"opinion," "notion"	"glory" of God (praise, radiance, effulgence), for Heb. *kavod*	"glory" of God or Christ	2 Cor. 3:18
ekklēsia	generic "assembly"	"gathering" of the people of Israel, for Heb. *qahal*	"church" as the gathering of saints	Matt. 16:18
episkeptomai	"review," "inspect"	sometimes for the eschatological "visitation" of God in judgment	often in the eschatological sense	Luke 1:68
euangelizomai	report of "good news" from battle	spiritual/salvific "good news," especially in Isaiah	"proclaiming the gospel"	Rom. 1:15

Table 6.1 (*continued*)

Word	Typical Secular Greek Use	Narrowing in the Greek OT	Influence on NT	Example
hilastērion	"expiation" (of the gods)	covering of the ark where atonement by blood is made, for Heb. *kapporet*	Jesus himself as the consummate "mercy seat" of propitiation	Rom. 3:25
kyrios	term of respect for anyone in authority	translation of "Lord" (both *adonai* and *kyrios*)*	titular for "Lord" Jesus	numerous
peri hamartias	"for sin"	technical term "sin offering," for Heb. *khatta't*	Jesus himself as the ultimate "sin offering"	Rom. 8:3
sklērokardia	(none)	newly coined for "hard-heartedness" of Israel, for Heb. "foreskin of heart"	spiritual hard-heartedness	Matt. 19:8

* The use of *kyrios* to translate YHWH is ubiquitous in the major codices of the Greek Old Testament, but other practices existed (such as * * * * in 4Q175, paleo-Hebrew lettering in 11Q5, and *IAŌ* in 4Q120). The use of *kyrios* by Philo (*Leg.* 1.48) and Josephus (*Ant.* 13.68–69) in Old Testament quotations where YHWH appears shows that the practice predates the New Testament.

One's Bible cannot help but influence his or her theological vocabulary, and this is just as true for early Christianity as it is today: "Any time a New Testament writer uses a term that is common in the LXX and that is closely associated with Hebrew theology, we may safely assume that what is said about that term's referent in the LXX would have significantly affected Christian reflection."[31]

Summary

A word of caution is in order: phrases and words do not become magical when they are used in the Bible, and one should avoid automatically importing a "Septuagintal meaning" or a "Hebrew concept" into the Greek style or vocabulary used in the New Testament.[32] The first port of call is always to study a given clause's meaning as it is used in the local New Testament context.

That said, the Greek Old Testament plays a valuable role in understanding the language of the New Testament, where one "is met at every turn by words and phrases which cannot be understood without reference to their earlier use in the Greek OT."[33] Regular reading of the Septuagint (even in translation) can help students grasp certain stylistic features of the New Testament. Moreover, studying a key word in a New Testament passage should always entail, if possible, exploring its use in the Greek Old Testament. This can be done by using software to look up specific instances of that word or by consulting a Septuagint-focused lexicon.[34] Doing either regularly will help the modern reader get a better sense for the theological dictionary of early Christianity.

---

31 Jobes and Silva, *Invitation*, 221.

32 See the cautions in Moisés Silva, *Biblical Words and Their Meaning: An Introduction to Lexical Semantics*, rev. ed. (Grand Rapids, MI: Zondervan, 1995).

33 Henry Barclay Swete, *An Introduction to the Old Testament in Greek* (Cambridge: Cambridge University Press, 1914), 404.

34 Takamitsu Muraoka, *A Greek-English Lexicon of the Septuagint: Chiefly of the Pentateuch and the Twelve Prophets* (Leuven: Peeters, 2009); Johan Lust, Erik Eynikel, and Katrin Hauspie, *Greek-English Lexicon of the Septuagint*, rev. ed. (Stuttgart: Deutsche Bibelgesellschaft, 2003).

The Use of the Greek Old Testament in the New Testament

Having previously outlined the evidence *that* the New Testament authors regularly use the Greek Old Testament, we now turn to *how* that influence plays out when the apostolic writers directly engage with this translation.

There is no question that the New Testament authors—following Jesus himself—treat old covenant Scriptures as directly inspired by God (Matt. 5:18; 2 Tim. 3:16; 1 Pet. 1:11; 2 Pet. 1:20–21). They quote or allude to the Old Testament hundreds of times and treat it as their touchstone for articulating the "gospel" (Rom. 1:2–4; Gal. 3:8) and the redemptive work of Christ (Luke 24:45–47; 1 Cor. 15:3–8). Few things are more important to understanding the theology of the New Testament than tracing its use of the Old Testament.[35] Indeed, some key points hang on the precise wording of an Old Testament passage (Gal. 3:16).

Because the translation of the Hebrew Bible into Greek was a generally stable endeavor, the wording available to the New Testament authors, whether in Hebrew or in Greek, is not noticeably different in many cases. But even casual attempts to look up Old Testament passages being quoted in the New Testament may reveal cases where the wording *does* differ. Sometimes this could be simply English-related translation issues or a tweak by the New Testament author to adapt a quotation to a new context. But the Greek Old Testament matters greatly because *sometimes New Testament authors make use of specific wording found in the Greek tradition of an Old Testament passage that differs meaningfully from the known Hebrew wording.* In such instances the Greek Old Testament plays a role in the formation of the New Testament's theology.

---

35 See Greg Lanier, *Old Made New: A Guide to the New Testament Use of the Old Testament* (Wheaton, IL: Crossway, forthcoming).

We analyze several examples here, across a variety of New Testament authors, to illustrate the point.[36] For each we provide the New Testament text and annotate it as follows: unmarked text indicates wording for which the Hebrew and traditional Old Greek text are essentially the same; bold text indicates places where the New Testament follows Old Greek wording in contrast to the Hebrew; brackets enclose clarifications.[37]

Gospels and Acts

MATTHEW 12:17–21 (ISAIAH 42:1–4)

This was to fulfill what was spoken by the prophet Isaiah:

"Behold, my servant whom I have chosen,
　my beloved with whom my soul is well pleased.
I will put my Spirit upon him,
　and he will proclaim justice to the Gentiles. . . .
　[A]nd in his name the Gentiles will hope [Heb. *And the
　coastlands wait for his law*]."

The wording of Matthew's quotation of Isaiah in Matthew 12:17–21 aligns with the Hebrew in omitting the Greek additions of "Israel" to "servant" and "Jacob" to "beloved." But in the final clause, he draws word for word on Old Greek Isaiah. The translator of Isaiah has, it seems, attempted to bring out an eschatological sense by swapping "Gentiles" (or "nations") for "coastlands." Matthew, then,

---

36　The bibliography for each passage discussed in this section is extensive and cannot be included here; for starters, see G. K. Beale and D. A. Carson, eds., *Commentary on the New Testament Use of the Old Testament* (Grand Rapids, MI: Baker Academic, 2007).

37　Unless otherwise noted, the New Testament is quoted from the ESV.

is able to make deft use of this difference in wording. The scene in question is Jesus's healing of a man on the Sabbath, which prompts scorn from the Jewish elite, who are quick to limit Jesus's ministry to strict Jewish boundaries. By drawing on the Old Greek form of the Isaiah passage, Matthew reminds us that even in the Old Testament, God's plan for his "servant" has always envisioned the inclusion of the Gentiles.

MARK 12:29–30 (DEUTERONOMY 6:4–5)

> Jesus answered, "The most important is, 'Hear, O Israel: The Lord our God, the Lord is one. And you shall love the Lord your God with all your heart and with all your soul **and with all your mind** [Heb. omits phrase] and with all your strength.'"

Mark 12 records Jesus's only quotation of the Jewish Shema in the Gospels.[38] Both textual traditions of Deuteronomy 6:5 include only three "with all your" clauses: Hebrew *heart, soul, strength*, and Old Greek *mind, soul, strength*.[39] The Markan account, however, includes four clauses. While on the surface it looks like Jesus (or Mark) is citing the Shema erroneously, a better explanation can be found. The Shema is repeated with different wording in the Old Testament itself (Josh. 22:5; 2 Kings 23:25), showing it to be a kind of living tradition that summarizes true piety. One Greek form of Joshua 22:5 contains "with all your mind," matching Mark. Thus, Mark's

---

38 See the detailed discussion in Martin Karrer, "The Septuagint Text in Early Christianity," in *Introduction to the LXX*, ed. Siegfried Kreuzer, trans. David A. Brenner and Peter Altmann (Waco, TX: Baylor University Press, 2019), 613–26.

39 This rendering follows the Göttingen reconstruction. *Septuaginta: Vetus Testamentum Graecum*, vol. 1, *Genesis*, ed. John W. Wevers (Göttingen: Vandenhoeck & Ruprecht, 1974); the Rahlfs-Hanhart edition reads, *heart, soul, strength*.

account is not in error but could be reflecting the broader Shema tradition[40] or combining the Hebrew and Old Greek forms of Deuteronomy 6:5.[41] In either case, the inclusion of the "mind" clause drives home the comprehensive love for God that characterizes Christian discipleship.

LUKE 3:35–36 (GENESIS 10:24)

... the son of Serug, the son of Reu, the son of Peleg, the son of Eber, the son of Shelah, **the son of Cainan** [Heb. omits phrase], the son of Arphaxad, the son of Shem, the son of Noah, the son of Lamech ...

Luke's genealogy in Luke 3:35–36 matches the Hebrew of Genesis spot-on except for the reference to "Cainan." One might be tempted to accuse Luke of making a mistake—that is, until consulting the Old Greek of Genesis 10:24, where we find "Arphaxad begat *Cainan*, and *Cainan* begat Shelah, and Shelah begat Eber." Clearly, Luke is using the Old Greek as his written source for the genealogy. It is possible that the Greek contains an earlier and better text and that somehow "Cainan" was accidentally lost in the Masoretic tradition.[42] Whatever the case, knowledge of the Greek Old Testament here clearly absolves Luke of any error.

LUKE 4:18–19 (ISAIAH 61:1–2)

The Spirit of the Lord is upon me,
  because **he** [Heb. *the LORD*] has anointed me

---

40 Mark's use of *ischyos* ("strength") instead of *dynameōs* (Deut. 6:5 OG) lends credence to this hypothesis, as it aligns with the Greek of 2 Kings [4 Kgdms.] 23:25.
41 Something similar happens with the addition of "do not defraud" in Mark 10:19.
42 Some English versions of Gen. 10:24 footnote the Greek addition of "Cainan."

to proclaim good news to the poor.

He has sent me [Heb./OG add *to bind up the brokenhearted,*] to
     proclaim liberty to the captives
and recovering of sight to the blind [Heb. omits phrase],
     to set at liberty those who are oppressed [Heb. *and the opening
         of the prison to those who are bound*; OG omits phrase],
to proclaim the year of the Lord's favor.

Luke's record of Jesus's sermon text at the Nazareth synagogue in Luke 4 has a complex relationship with the Greek and Hebrew wording of Isaiah 61. Three things particularly stand out.

First, the clause "to bind up the brokenhearted" found in both the Hebrew and Old Greek is absent in Luke. Second, "recovering of sight to the blind" does not have a direct match in the Hebrew but matches the Old Greek verbatim.[43] Third, "set at liberty those who are oppressed" is absent in the Old Greek of Isaiah 61:1 but almost exactly matches the Greek of Isaiah 58:6; its inclusion here may stem from the thematic similarities of Isaiah 58 and 61 as well as from the phrase's resemblance to "opening of the prison to those who are bound" in the Hebrew of Isaiah 61:1.

There is no established consensus that accounts for all the data. Perhaps the Nazareth scroll deviates from what becomes the Masoretic tradition; perhaps Jesus or Luke are relying more heavily on a Greek form of Isaiah. Whatever the case, the Old Greek of Isaiah—especially "recovering of sight to the blind"—is important for Luke's strategic use

---

43 Some suggest that the Old Greek "recovering of sight to the blind" is a paraphrase of the Hebrew "opening of the prison to those who are bound"; this seems unlikely, but even if it were, our broader point remains unchanged: Luke's account is still drawing word for word here on the Old Greek, not the Hebrew.

of this Nazareth scene:[44] it tightly connects the sermon with Jesus's ministry of physical healing that was already unfolding in Galilee. Through his miraculous deeds, Jesus proves that he is the Spirit-filled one anticipated by Isaiah (Luke 4:21).

ACTS 7:14 (GENESIS 46:27)

Joseph sent and summoned Jacob his father and all his kindred, **seventy-five** [Heb. *seventy*] persons in all.

One might be tempted to accuse Luke of misquoting the number of people who went to Egypt in Acts 7:14, since modern English translations read, "seventy" (from the Hebrew), versus Luke's "seventy-five." But Luke again has simply followed his Greek Genesis text. The bigger question is why there is a difference between the Hebrew and the Old Greek in the first place. Most likely this variation derives from different ways of counting the descendants.[45] The Old Greek of Deuteronomy 10:22, in fact, reads, "seventy," in line with the Hebrew. Both numbers are "correct," depending on how you draw the family tree. Knowing this detail via the Greek Old Testament clears away skepticism about Luke's accuracy.

ACTS 15:15–18 (AMOS 9:11–12)

And with this the words of the prophets agree, just as it is written,

---

44 Luke has shifted this scene forward in the time line relative to Mark 6 and Matt. 13 to give it a programmatic significance.

45 There are a few possible ways to do the math. One can arrive at seventy by adding sixty-six (the biological descendants tabulated in Gen. 46:8–25 and restated in 46:26) and four (Jacob, Leah, Zilpah, Bilhah). One can arrive at seventy-five by adding sixty-six (from above) and nine (the full number of Joseph's children born in Egypt, i.e., Ephraim and Manasseh plus seven others, as summarized in the Greek version of Gen. 46:27).

"After this I will return [Heb./OG *In that day*],
and I will rebuild the tent of David that has fallen;
I will rebuild its ruins,

    and I will restore it [Heb./OG add *as in the days of old*],
that the remnant of mankind may seek the Lord [Heb. *they*
        may possess the remnant of Edom],
    and all the Gentiles who are called by my name."

James's citation of Amos in Acts 15:15–18 serves as the decisive scriptural testimony in the Jerusalem Council. The wording of James's quotation has several minor differences relative to the Hebrew and Greek forms of Amos 9 (not all indicated here).[46] The most significant observation is that the quotation follows the Old Greek wording "that the remnant of mankind may seek the Lord." Several questions arise. Did Luke supply this rendering from his copy of Greek Amos, or did James specifically quote this form at the council? Was there a Hebrew text that read something like this in contrast to the Masoretic Text we know today, or did the Greek wording emerge via exegetical interpretation?[47] Multiple explanations are viable.

What is clear, though, is that the Greek form solidifies the connection James is making at this decisive moment in redemptive history. As God has spoken in the prophets, the "rebuilding" of new Israel under a new "David" does not stop with Jews but expands to the whole

---

46 See Wolfgang Kraus, "The Role of the Septuagint in the New Testament: Amos 9:11–12 as a Test Case," in *Translation Is Required: The Septuagint in Retrospect and Prospect*, ed. Robert J. V. Hiebert, SCS 56 (Atlanta: SBL, 2010), 171–90.

47 "Edom" is close to "man" in Hebrew; moreover, "seek" and "possess" differ by only one letter in Hebrew.

world, so that the faithful remnant of all mankind, from every nation, can be part of God's people by seeking the Lord.

Epistles and Revelation

ROMANS 11:26–27 (ISAIAH 59:20–21)

And in this way all Israel will be saved, as it is written,

> "The Deliverer will come from [Heb. *to*; OG *on behalf of*] Zion,
>   **he will banish ungodliness from Jacob** [Heb. *to those in*
>   *Jacob who turn from transgression*];
>   and this will be my covenant with them
>   when I take away their sins."

At the crescendo of Paul's discussion about Israel's future and the ingrafting of Gentiles in Romans 11, he quotes Isaiah 59:20–21. The first notable feature of this quotation is how the deliverer figure will come "from" Zion, which contrasts with both Hebrew and Old Greek forms. Paul appears to be making a subtle update in light of the unfolding timeline of God's saving plan, possibly pointing forward to Jesus's (or the Father's) coming *from* heavenly "Zion."

The second feature involves Paul's reliance on the Old Greek description of this deliverer's action when he comes. The Hebrew places the onus on Israelite repentance; the Greek shifts the onus to the deliverer, who himself will turn away their sin. While both are true—Paul certainly emphasizes personal repentance in Romans—the Old Greek text of Isaiah serves his purpose better at this stage in his argument, since it places the weight on the eschatological work of Christ.

ROMANS 14:10–11 (ISAIAH 45:23)

For we will all stand before the judgment seat of God; for it is written,

> "As I live, says the Lord, every knee shall bow to me,
>> and every tongue shall **confess to God** [Heb. *swear allegiance*]."

At the end of Romans 14, Paul exhorts Christians not to pass judgment against one another in debatable matters, for there is a greater Judge. He defends this principle by quoting the Old Greek of Isaiah 45. His readers have already "sworn allegiance" to God, so the Hebrew wording is less salient. The issue is, rather, that even Christians will "give an account . . . to God" (Rom. 14:12). Thus, the wording "confess to God" serves his point better: not only will Christians bow to the Lord, but they will confess before his eschatological judgment seat as well. Therefore, we should avoid being judgmental now.

ROMANS 15:12 (ISAIAH 11:10)

And again Isaiah says,

> "The root of Jesse will come,
>> even he **who arises to rule the Gentiles** [Heb. *who shall stand as a signal for the peoples*];
>> **in him will the Gentiles hope** [Heb. *of him shall the nations inquire*]."

Prior to his closing greetings in Romans, Paul quotes a series of Old Testament passages that support the epistle's Jew-Gentile theme. The Old Greek of Isaiah 11:10 more readily allows Paul to establish Jesus, the

Jewish "root of Jesse," as one who will "arise" not just as a signal flag but as a "ruler" over Gentiles as well as Jews, reflecting a point from Romans 3:29. Moreover, the idea of the Gentiles "hoping" in Christ fits a key theme in Romans (5:2–4; 8:20–24) better than the Hebrew "inquire."

1 CORINTHIANS 2:16 (ISAIAH 40:13)

"For who has **understood the mind** [Heb. *measured the Spirit*] of the Lord so as to instruct him?" But we have the mind of Christ.

In the broader context of 1 Corinthians 1–2, Paul contrasts worldly wisdom with Christian wisdom. He proves it by quoting Isaiah 40:13, using the Old Greek "mind" (*nous*) instead of the Hebrew "Spirit."[48] Though both forms of Isaiah 40:13 emphasize that mere man cannot probe the inner life of God, the Greek Old Testament here better suits Paul's argument. In contrast to the world, Christians have the indwelling "Spirit" of God (already introduced in 1 Cor. 2:10–13) and thus can understand the revealed "mind" of God—insofar as we are conformed in "mind" to Christ.[49]

GALATIANS 3:19 AND HEBREWS 2:2 (DEUTERONOMY 33:2)

Why then the law? . . . It was put in place through **angels** by an intermediary. (Gal. 3:19)

For since the message declared by **angels** proved to be reliable . . . (Heb. 2:2)

---

48 The same phrasing appears in Rom. 11:34; Aquila and Symmachus read, "Spirit" (Gk. *pneuma*), for Isa. 40:13.

49 See McLay, *Use of the Septuagint*, 150–53.

Both Galatians 3:19 and Hebrews 2:2 speak of the giving of the Torah via angels (also Acts 7:53). A glance at Exodus 19–20 and Deuteronomy 5 confirms that the Hebrew Bible does not explicitly record the presence of angels at Sinai with Moses when he received the law. Some argue that the New Testament authors are drawing on a Jewish tradition here.[50] Though possible, the more likely explanation is that Paul and the author of Hebrews are alluding to the Greek wording found in Deuteronomy 33:2. While the Hebrew describes the Lord at Sinai with "ten thousand holy ones," the Old Greek describes "angels with him at his right hand"—a detail to which the New Testament authors seem to be alluding.

HEBREWS 1:6 (DEUTERONOMY 32:43)

Again, when he brings the firstborn into the world, he says,

"Let all God's angels worship him [Heb. omits phrase]."

Hebrews 1:5–14 draws on multiple Old Testament passages to make exalted claims about Jesus's divinity. Hebrews 1:6 is one of the most impressive, as the Father commands even angels to worship his "firstborn" son—a status no mere human could enjoy. But the quoted text is drawn from the longer Greek of Deuteronomy 32:43 and is not present in the Masoretic Text (recall table 5.3 in chap. 5). A portion is also attested in 4Q44 of the Dead Sea Scrolls. Thus, the Old Greek wording used in Hebrews may reflect an earlier and better text than the shorter Masoretic Text form (which is why some modern Bibles like the ESV present a composite form at Deut. 32:43). Whatever

---

50 E.g., Jub. 1.26–28; 2.1; Josephus, *Ant.* 15.136; Philo, *Somn.* 1.141–43.

the case, this additional wording from Moses's final song allows the author to drive home the huge difference between Jesus and angels.

HEBREWS 10:5–6 (PSALM 40[39]:6[7])

Consequently, when Christ came into the world, he said,

> "Sacrifices and offerings you have not desired,
>> but **a body have you prepared for me** [Heb. *but you have given me an open ear*];[51]
> in burnt offerings and sin offerings
> you have taken no pleasure."

The Masoretic Text of this psalm uses an "ear" metaphor that either evokes the piercing of a slave's ear to assign him to his master (Ex. 21:6) or portrays the psalmist's desire for an ear that will obey the Lord. While some ancient versions of the psalm likewise use the "ear" phrasing,[52] most existing Greek Old Testament manuscripts contain the "body" phrase that the author of Hebrews uses.[53] Scholars continue to debate how the two alternatives ("ear" versus "body") came about; either the Greek translator of Psalm 40 had a different Hebrew text in front of him, or someone along the way updated the metaphor in Greek for rhetorical reasons.[54]

However it came about, the Greek "body" is essential to the point in Hebrews. The author is arguing that the repeated "offerings" of

---

51 More woodenly, "ears you have dug for me."
52 E.g., Gallican Psalter, Aquila, Symmachus, Theodotion.
53 Notably, the Göttingen edition of the Greek psalter emends the text to "ears" despite little manuscript evidence for it.
54 See Karen H. Jobes, "Rhetorical Achievement in the Hebrews 10 'Misquote' of Psalm 40," *Bib* 72, no. 3 (1991): 387–96.

animal bodies in Israel's temple system have been consummated in the singular sacrifice of Christ's "body." This self-offering of his own physical "body" is the key reason he "came into the world" in the incarnation (Heb. 10:5).

HEBREWS 10:37–38 (HABAKKUK 2:3–4)

Yet a little while,

and **the coming one** [Heb. *it*] will come and will not delay;

but **my righteous one** [Heb. *the righteous*] shall live by faith,

and if he shrinks back,

my soul has no pleasure in him [Heb. *Behold, his soul is puffed up; it is not upright within him*].

In Romans 1:17 and Galatians 3:11, Habakkuk 2:3–4 helps Paul summarize the gospel, connecting "righteousness" with "faith." But the same passage is put to different use in Hebrews, expedited by specific details in the Greek Old Testament.[55] First, the Old Greek wording of Habakkuk 2:3 helps the author connect directly to Christ as "the coming one" who will dispense an eternal reward (Heb. 10:35–36). Second, the Old Greek wording enables Hebrews to apply Habakkuk 2:4 to the Christian's endurance "by faith." The one who has already been made righteous by God ("my righteous one") shall endure by faith as well, refusing to "shrink back" (Heb. 10:39). The Greek of Habakkuk's prophecy, in other words, performs double duty in the New Testament. It supports Paul's doctrine of justification (faith as

---

55 See Wolfgang Kraus, "Hab 2:3–4 in the Hebrew Tradition and in the Septuagint, with Its Reception in the New Testament," in *Septuagint and Reception: Essays Prepared for the Association for the Study of the Septuagint in South Africa*, ed. Johann Cook, VTSup 127 (Leiden: Brill, 2009), 101–18.

instrument of righteousness) *and* Hebrew's doctrine of endurance (faith as that which sustains).

REVELATION 2:26–27 (PSALM 2:9)

> The one who conquers and who keeps my works until the end, to him I will give authority over the nations, and he will **shepherd** [ESV mg.; Heb. *break*] them with a rod of iron, as when earthen pots are broken in pieces, even as I myself have received authority from my Father.[56]

The wording of the allusion to Psalm 2:9 in Revelation 2:26–27 agrees with the Old Greek ("shepherd") against the Hebrew ("break"). The Hebrew is more violent and would surely fit with Revelation's motifs. But the adoption of the Old Greek allows John to connect the Old Testament motif of the Davidic Messiah as eschatological "shepherd" (e.g., Ezek. 34:23–24) with Jesus as slain "Lamb." John combines these images in Revelation 7:17, where the "Lamb" takes the throne to "shepherd" the saints. But John does not stop there. He alludes to this Greek form of Psalm 2:9 twice more (Rev. 12:5; 19:15) to show that Jesus will "shepherd with a rod of iron" not only Israel but, in fact, all Gentile "nations."

Summary

We could add other examples where New Testament authors lean in the direction of the Greek Old Testament and away from the traditional Hebrew text, but these suffice to establish the point. In both minor and major ways, the Greek tradition (typically the Old Greek)

---

56 The ESV reads, "he will rule them with a rod of iron," but the Greek *poimanei* is better rendered "he will shepherd."

has exerted discernible influence on New Testament theology through Greek translators' exegesis of the Old Testament. The Greek Old Testament matters to today's reader, then, because it is often essential to understanding the point the apostolic authors are making.

Concluding Thoughts

The aim of this chapter has been to introduce the reader to the significance of the Greek Old Testament (or "Septuagint") for the task of studying the New Testament. We conclude with a few lines of application that draw together the key points of this chapter.

First, interpreters need to handle quotations of the Old Testament in the New Testament case by case and need to include all the evidence. Many factors come into play when tracing the use of the Old Testament in the New Testament. The New Testament author may be drawing on a known Hebrew form, a known Greek form, or some combination. And wording variations could arise through quoting from memory, from oral tradition, or from some source no longer available to us. Sometimes the relationship between the New Testament and the Old Testament passage being quoted is straightforward, but other times it is not. Thus, we encourage today's students of the Bible to handle each instance separately, factoring in all the evidence—not the least of which is the Greek Old Testament—to ensure that they capture the New Testament author's point. This requires more labor, but the result is worth it.

Second, broad reading in the Greek Old Testament helps sharpen the New Testament student's exegetical skills. One temptation every reader of the New Testament faces is "overexegesis"—that is, squeezing every drop of significance out of a given noun, preposition, verb, or syntactical feature. This likely stems from the (mis)conception that the

Greek is some kind of magic decoder ring. One way to guard against this temptation is to read the Greek Old Testament, which reflects the language of the New Testament era and, as shown, directly affects it. By regular exposure to the Greek Old Testament either directly (preferable) or in English (if needed),[57] one learns how to approach words and phrases in the New Testament more soberly.[58]

But the opposite is also true: exposure to the Greek Old Testament can alert the reader when a word or phrase in the New Testament *is* noteworthy, so as to avoid "underexegesis." For example, some translations of Matthew 2:2 state that the nativity "star" was seen "in the east," implying that it is simply a geographic detail. But someone familiar with the Greek Old Testament will realize that "in its rising" is better. Why? Because Matthew is alluding to the Greek wording of Balaam's oracle (Num. 24:17), which describes the promised king of Israel as a "star [who] shall rise." Consequently, hearing this "Septuagintal" ring of a "rising star" helps the reader grasp the fuller significance of Matthew's phrasing—and understand why the magi sought Israel's new king in the first place. The Greek Old Testament, in other words, can be a first port of call in understanding the nuances of meaning of many key words or phrases in the New Testament.

Third, the New Testament authors' use of the Greek Old Testament—even citing it as "Scripture"—warrants serious reflection. The Greek Old Testament was (with caveats) a "pew Bible" of the apostolic church. But as covered in both chapter 5 and this chapter, its wording

---

57 Through the New English Translation of the Septuagint (NETS) or the Lexham English Septuagint (LES).

58 A great example is the oft-abused aorist verb. Encountering over forty-nine thousand of these in the Greek Old Testament helps readers avoid overloading any given aorist in the New Testament with too much freight.

does not always align with the Hebrew that is the basis of today's translations. And in many cases this different wording is cited *as Scripture* by the New Testament authors. For instance, Hebrews 3:7 begins a quote of Psalm 95[94]:7–11 with "The Holy Spirit says"—a rather high claim—and then proceeds to use the *Greek* form that differs four times from the traditional Hebrew. This raises many important questions. Which form is directly inspired? Which is authoritative? How should the church approach the Greek Old Testament today in light of the New Testament authors' regular use of it? Such questions require careful consideration. Thus, we devote the next chapter to them.

7

What Kind of Authority Does the Septuagint Have?

WE HAVE ARRIVED AT WHAT IS, in many respects, the most important chapter of this book. Thus far, we have surveyed complex data regarding the Greek Old Testament. We have seen that many ancient manuscripts include Apocryphal books that are adopted by the Roman Catholic and Orthodox Churches but not by Protestants (or Jews). We have shown where the shape or specific wording of books differs between the Greek and Hebrew. We have seen that the New Testament authors frequently quote the Greek Old Testament, even when it differs from the Hebrew we use today.

It is time to discuss the implications. What should we do with the "Septuagint" today? Or, more precisely, how should the church's doctrine of the nature of Scripture incorporate the Greek Old Testament, if at all? Or, more precisely still, does the Greek Old Testament have any *authority* today?

With respect to this question, a polarity has emerged in recent decades as the academic interest in the Greek Old Testament has trickled into the church. One pole argues that today's Protestant church should (like the Orthodox Church) downgrade, or even abandon, its adherence to the Masoretic Hebrew and adopt the "Septuagint" as its authoritative Old Testament text.[1] The basic reason is this: if the apostles and early church used the "Septuagint" as the primary text of the new covenant era instead of going back to the Hebrew of its Jewish roots, then today's church should too.

The other pole is one of either silence on or unawareness of the Greek Old Testament altogether. This is certainly the case at the layperson level—indeed, addressing this gap was one of our core motivations for writing this book. But it extends beyond that, as represented vividly by the fact that the ~1,200-page book billed as the decisive treatment of scriptural authority by a "veritable who's who of evangelical scholars" mentions the issues related to the Greek Old Testament on only two pages of one essay.[2]

So which is it? Should the "Septuagint" have full authority as the Old Testament of today's church?[3] Or should its authority at best get buried

---

1 Articulated, for instance, in Robert W. Funk, "The Once and Future New Testament," in *The Canon Debate*, ed. Lee Martin McDonald and James A. Sanders (Peabody, MA: Hendrickson, 2002), 541–57, esp. 542, 546; Møgens Müller, "The Septuagint as the Bible of the New Testament Church: Some Reflections," *SJOT* 7, no. 2 (1993): 194–207; Müller, *The First Bible of the Church: A Plea for the Septuagint*, JSOTSup 206 (Sheffield: Sheffield Academic Press, 1996); Martin Hengel, *The Septuagint as Christian Scripture: Its Prehistory and the Problem of Its Canon* (Edinburgh: T&T Clark, 2002).

2 D. A. Carson, ed., *The Enduring Authority of the Christian Scriptures* (Grand Rapids, MI: Eerdmans, 2016); "who's who" is from the back cover. The essay in mind is Stephen J. Dempster, "The Old Testament Canon, Josephus, and Cognitive Environment," 321–61. Surprisingly, the "Septuagint" is barely mentioned in the essay titled "The Problem of the New Testament's Use of the Old Testament," by Douglas J. Moo and Andrew David Naselli, 702–46, which focuses almost exclusively on hermeneutics. Our point is not to condemn the book but to point out what would seem to be a glaring omission.

3 We lay aside both ancient and neo-Marcionism, which deny that the Old Testament has any real bearing on today's church at all.

in the footnotes? And if the right answer is somewhere in between, how can we better articulate the place of the Greek Old Testament in our doctrine of Scripture?

We will approach this issue by attempting to bring much-needed precision to the discussion of "authority" itself, which for these purposes is defined (imperfectly) as *the way a text declares and enforces truth within a community of faith.* We will outline three different forms of authority, as summarized in table 7.1, and will then articulate how the Greek Old Testament fits into the picture.

Table 7.1   Framework for "Authority"

Normative	Derivative	Interpretive
That which is Scripture, revelation directly inspired by God through human authors and used to adjudicate matters of faith and practice	That which plays a rightful role as the word of God for specific communities of the church, expressly derived from the normative Scripture	That which plays the role of an illuminating and edifying commentary on Scripture, as part of broader church tradition

One could say that normative authority deals with the *words* (or *text*) of Scripture as given, while derivative authority deals with capturing and conveying its *meaning*—with interpretive authority being even further downstream from there.

To use a simple analogy, a parent's house rule "Curfew is at 10 p.m." has normative authority. A translation of its wording for a foreign-exchange student living with the family ("El toque de queda de casa es a las 10 p.m.") would possess derivative authority, in that it is derived from and captures the meaning of what the parents declare but is not verbatim identical with it. And one sibling's reminder to another—"Be home by 10 p.m.!"—would possess interpretive authority.

Normative Authority

From the time of ancient Israel to the apostolic church, the place where normative authority was seen to reside was the directly inspired speech-act of God recorded by men in what we designate (for clarity's sake) *Scripture(s)*. The Old Testament aptly describes this collection of writings as "the law and the words that the LORD of hosts had sent by his Spirit through the former prophets" (Zech. 7:12). The New Testament in turn describes such Scriptures as "breathed out by God and profitable" (2 Tim. 3:16) and as given directly by the Spirit of God through the prophets of old (e.g., Luke 1:70; 1 Pet. 1:10–12).

The question, then, is this: Where is such normative Scripture to be found? We argue that all evidence points toward the Hebrew Bible, in terms of both canon (which books) and text (the wording of those books, as best as we can reconstruct). The Greek Old Testament—however valuable it may be to the task of unlocking the history of the Hebrew Bible—should not supplant it as that which bears normative authority.

Canon

Let us pick up where we left off in chapter 5, in the discussion of the "boundaries" of the Old Testament. We can be more precise now in defining *canon* as the collection of books received by the people of God as bearing normative authority. While Judaism, Protestantism, Roman Catholicism, and Orthodoxy fully align on a core set of books (Genesis–Malachi), the latter two faith traditions incorporate other books, such as 1–2 Maccabees and Tobit, as a "second canon" largely because they are included in the budding Greek corpus of Jewish writings. Some argue that the mere existence of multiple "canons" means the whole issue is open ended—if so, why not embrace these books of the Apocrypha?

This approach, however, confuses *Scripture* with *canon*. Scripture, as the inspired record of God's speech-acts, simply *is*. But canon is the result of a (potentially) fallible human process of *discerning* what should be acknowledged as Scripture.[4] And as such, a canon list can be judged "right" or "wrong" to the extent that it accurately discerns what is and is not Scripture.[5] On this point, the traditional threefold Hebrew canon shared by all traditions has the weight of historical evidence in its favor, while the larger so-called "Septuagintal" or "Alexandrian" canon that includes the Apocrypha does not.

EMERGENCE OF THE THREEFOLD HEBREW CANON

A threefold collection of Scripture—Law (Torah or Pentateuch), Prophets, and Writings[6]—began emerging even in biblical times. Later books regularly reference the "Law of Moses" (e.g., Josh. 8:31–32) and quote specifically from Genesis–Deuteronomy (e.g., 2 Kings 14:6). Similarly, books that belong to the Prophets are cited elsewhere in the Old Testament, such as Jeremiah's use of Micah (Jer. 26:16–18)

---

4 On distinguishing Scripture (as intrinsic "religious authority") and canon (as extrinsic "listing of the Scriptures"), see Tomas Bokedal, *The Formation and Significance of the Christian Biblical Canon: A Study in Text, Ritual, and Interpretation* (London: Bloomsbury, 2014), 18.

5 One major distinction between the Reformed/Protestant and Roman Catholic positions is that the former affirms that through the self-authentication of Scripture and the guidance of the Holy Spirit (not papal fiat or council decision), the church has *rightly* received the canonical books.

6 In Hebrew, *Torah*, *Nevi'im*, and *Ketuvim* (in short, Tanak).

or Ezra's and Daniel's use of Jeremiah (Ezra 1:1; Dan. 9:2), and some of the Writings are referenced or reused in other books (e.g., 1 Kings 4:32). Moreover, Zechariah refers to "law" and "former prophets" (Zech. 7:12), while a rough threefold shape ("law," "prophets," and "counsel") appears to lie behind Jeremiah 18:18 and Ezekiel 7:26.

The threefold canonical awareness crystallizes in the Second Temple period. The prologue to the book of Ben Sira is the earliest reference: "Many great teachings have been given to us through the *law* and the *prophets* and the *others* that followed them." Similar statements can be found in the Dead Sea Scrolls (4Q397 frag. 14–21); 2 Maccabees 2:13–14; 4 Maccabees 18:10–18; Philo, *De vita contemplativa*, 25; and Josephus, *Against Apion*, 1.38–14. Though the nomenclature for the Writings is not yet standardized in this period, the basic three divisions are visible. The threefold collection receives its clearest Jewish endorsement in the Talmud (*B. Bat.* 14b, a tannaitic saying from roughly AD 150–180).

Turning to the New Testament, we find numerous references to "the Law and the Prophets" (e.g., Matt. 5:17; 7:12; 11:13; 22:40; John 1:45; Acts 13:15) as well as multiple quotations from all three divisions. But the defining statement is found in Jesus's teaching on the Emmaus Road: "Everything written about me in the *Law of Moses* and the *Prophets* and the *Psalms* must be fulfilled" (Luke 24:44).[7] In all their debates with Jewish teachers on how to interpret the Old Testament, Jesus and Paul never dispute its canonical boundaries. All evidence suggests that the earliest Christian community adopted the Jewish threefold canon—why would they not, given their Jewish roots?

No doubt there was debate over whether certain books should be considered part of this threefold collection (notably Esther, Ecclesi-

---

7 "Psalms" here is likely a synecdoche for the Writings.

astes, and Song of Songs). But the framework of the threefold Law, Prophets, and Writings *as Scripture*—including a stable core of specific books—is never itself in dispute in earliest Judaism and Christianity.

THE "ALEXANDRIAN" CANON MYTH

The fly in the ointment is, of course, the early debates on the Apocrypha. These writings were attached at the hip, it seems, to the Greek Old Testament corpus, leading to their inclusion in later codices. As a result, some scholars have postulated that the narrower threefold Hebrew canon held sway in Palestine but that the expanded canon held sway in Egypt. The syllogism would run thus: since early Christianity makes use of the Greek Old Testament text of Alexandria, it implicitly endorses its canon too.[8] This logic, combined with the fact that many churches *were* indeed putting the Apocrypha to use, led to Augustine's pro-Apocrypha stance, which was redressed, in time, by Jerome. The Protestant church followed the latter, and two lines of argument suggest that this was the right move.

First, there are intrinsic reasons to reject the "Alexandrian" canon. The canonical mindset of both Judaism and Christianity holds that Scripture is documentation of God's covenant with Israel; we see this in the Old Testament itself (Ex. 31:18; Ps. 50:16), Jewish writings (Sir. 24:23; 1 Macc. 1:56–67), and church fathers (Origen, *Comm. Jo.* 5.4; Eusebius, *Hist. eccl.* 3.9.5). On top of this, covenantal Scripture is given by God only during the era of prophetic activity in Israel. But in the

---

8 Karen Jobes states that this syllogism is one of the reasons Protestants tend to be skittish about the Greek Old Testament. "When God Spoke Greek: The Place of the Greek Bible in Evangelical Scholarship," *BBR* 16, no. 2 (2006): 219–36. To be clear, some proponents of adopting the Septuagint today stop short of adopting the Apocrypha (e.g., Hengel).

period after Ezra and Nehemiah, Israel remains largely dispersed in the exilic state of covenant curse (e.g., James 1:1; 1 Pet. 1:1), with the word of authorized prophets ceasing after Malachi.[9] As such, any later writings like the Apocrypha could not, by definition, be considered covenantal or prophetic.[10]

Second, there are extrinsic reasons to reject the "Alexandrian" canon. There is no concrete evidence that the Jews in Egypt drew canonical boundaries differently than their counterparts in Israel did.[11] Moreover, despite Alexandria's importance, Jerusalem remained the center of gravity within Judaism until AD 70. If the apostolic movement were to take direction on its Old Testament canon from somewhere, it would be Jerusalem, not Alexandria. The inclusion of various Apocryphal books in Greek biblical codices simply reflects the reading habits of the Christians that produced them—some of the same codices include the Shepherd of Hermas and 1 Clement too—and likely does not reflect the canon of Alexandria hundreds of years prior. Even today the inclusion of essays, concordances, and maps in study Bibles does not mean those items are equivalent to the canonical writings.

In short, the strongest evidence suggests that normative Scripture is contained only in the threefold Hebrew collection of books.

Text

Even if we set aside the Apocrypha as having any viable claim to normative authority, there still remains an important question:

---

9 See 1 Macc. 4:46; Pr. Azar. 15; Josephus, *Ag. Ap.* 1.8; 2 Bar. 85.2; Heb. 1:1.

10 On this, see Robert Hanhart's prologue to Hengel, *Septuagint*, 3. Some also defend the Hebrew canon based on the language of composition, but this line of reasoning is weakened by the fact that other Jewish writings, including some Apocryphal books, originated in Hebrew.

11 As even Müller acknowledges, *First Bible*, 39–40.

Which *text* of the canonical books is normative, the Hebrew or the Greek? Paying careful attention to our definitions, it is clear that the Hebrew text, as reconstructed to the best of our ability using the Masoretic tradition as well as other evidence, is the normative authority for today's church. This is not changed by the fact that some Jews, New Testament authors, and early Christians used the Greek Old Testament—we return to that below. Let us explore why this is the case.

THE EXISTENCE OF A STANDARD TEXT

It is certainly true, as outlined in prior chapters, that the Old Greek tradition—as well as other revisions of the Greek, the Dead Sea Scrolls, the Samaritan Pentateuch, and so on—complicate the story of how the Old Testament came down to us. Even the footnotes of modern English translations admit this (e.g., the ESV notes for Deut. 32). The existence of such complexity has led to the rise of a particular critical portrait of this process: textual plurality goes all the way back to ancient Israel, as different variants of most biblical books circulated with little concern for consistency from the beginning. Only when the dust settled after AD 135 did one main Jewish group (Pharisees) and one textual tradition emerge, which eventually became the Masoretic Text.[12] If this is the case, the argument goes, then Christianity, birthed before the emergence of a standardized Hebrew text, might as well adopt the "Septuagint" text of the apostles as its normative authority, not the Hebrew.

A more accurate portrait is as follows, picking up some threads from chapter 1. As the scribes of Israel recorded the normative

---

12 As argued by Timothy M. Law, *When God Spoke Greek: The Septuagint and the Making of the Christian Bible* (Oxford: Oxford University Press, 2013).

Scriptures, copies were housed first in the ark of the covenant (Ex. 25:16; Deut. 10:1–5; 31:24–26),[13] then in the temple precincts (1 Sam. 10:25; 2 Kings 22:8; Josephus, *Ant.* 3.1.7; 5.1.17; Let. Aris. 176; 1 Macc. 1:54–57; 2 Macc. 2:13–14), and finally in scroll cabinets of the synagogues that emerged during the postexilic period (Philo, *Contempl.* 25; Luke 4:16–20). The priests associated with the temple archive thus played the decisive function of adjudicating not only which scrolls belonged (the canon question) but also the text of each as, over time, they were copied (Deut. 17:18–19) and fine-tuned (Jer. 36:32), culminating in an authorized form. This centralized temple function was no different from how other ancient people groups transmitted their sacred writings.[14] In short, the royal scribes and priests stewarded a standard Hebrew text long before the first century.

The complexity enters the picture in the tumultuous time during and after the exile. The priests, scribes, and other educated Jews scattered to Babylonia and (later) throughout the Persian and Greek Empires (2 Kings 24:14–15; Jer. 24:1). The Hebrew Bible went with them. The process of copying, reading, and eventually translating what was once an essentially standardized text began to introduce local variations, both large and small. In such a volatile environment, it is actually surprising—considering this was long before the printing press or computer—that there is not *more* variation than what we do find.

13 David M. Carr, *Writing on the Tablet of the Heart: Origins of Scripture and Literature* (Oxford: Oxford University Press, 2005), 160–61.

14 Summarized in Peter J. Gentry, "MasPs[a] and the Early History of the Hebrew Psalter: Notes on Canon and Text," in *Studies on the Intersection of Text, Paratext, and Reception: A Festschrift in Honor of Charles E. Hill*, ed. Gregory R. Lanier and J. Nicholas Reid, TENTS 15 (Leiden: Brill, 2021).

When the temple was reconstructed under Ezra and Nehemiah, it resumed its function as an archive where priestly scribes preserved and transmitted the "master version" of the Hebrew text (e.g., 2 Macc. 2:13–14; Josephus, *Ant.* 3.38; 4.303; 5.61).[15] The existence of this standard is further indicated by the family of texts discovered in the Judean Desert that scholars classify as a "proto–Masoretic Text." Amid an environment of otherwise nonstandard texts discovered around the Dead Sea, these manuscripts were apparently normed by the authoritative, standard text.[16]

Thus, the Masoretic tradition is the endpoint of a process of preserving the normative text that started centuries earlier. Though imperfect—even the Masoretes admit as much with their annotations—it remains a remarkably good starting point for reconstructing the standard temple text.

In short, there is clear evidence amid the later textual variety for an authoritative and largely fixed text of the Hebrew Bible, which was standardized at least by the second century BC and associated with the Jerusalem temple. If the textual tradition is a river, we should view it as a singular river that later branched out, rather than numerous independent headwaters that were eventually forced into a canal.

---

15 See the discussion of rabbinical attestation of the "master copy" and official scribal "correctors" in Emanuel Tov, "The Text of the Hebrew/Aramaic and Greek Bible Used in the Ancient Synagogues," in *Hebrew Bible, Greek Bible, and Qumran: Collected Essays*, TSAJ 121 (Tübingen: Mohr Siebeck, 2008), 177–80. See also Peter J. Gentry, "The Text of the Old Testament," *JETS* 52, no. 1 (2009): 19–45.

16 Tov, "Text," 179–81. Many Qumran scrolls preserve a text that is quite close to the proto–Masoretic Text but almost never as precisely similar as texts from other sites in the Judean Desert, such as Masada and Muraba'at, all of which are in fact essentially identical to the Leningrad Codex, which serves as the basis of modern critical editions of the Hebrew Bible. Tov, "Text," 176.

THE EXISTENCE AND EDITING OF THE GREEK OLD TESTAMENT

While this seems obvious, it often gets lost in the discussion: the sheer fact that the "Septuagint" is a collection of translations of the Hebrew source text points to the primacy of that source. When translating, the goal is not to supplant the source wholesale but to give access to it. Not only this, but the subsequent editorial work on the Greek translations—the Kaige movement as well as the recensions by Aquila, Symmachus, and Theodotion—all tend to revise toward the Hebrew. It was the norm by which the Greek traditions were modified, not the other way around.

THE USE OF THE GREEK OLD TESTAMENT AS A CONDUIT TO THE HEBREW

Though the intentions of the Letter of Aristeas remain debated (see chap. 2), it is important to recognize that the author defends the "Septuagint," at least in part, because he believed that it exactly corresponded to the Hebrew and thus conveys its authority. He cites a correspondence to the king that states, "The books of the law of the Jews . . . are written in the Hebrew characters and language and have been carelessly interpreted, and do not represent the original text."[17] The resulting translation would, by fixing this problem, point not to its own authority alone but to that of the normative Hebrew original.

Something similar is true in the early church, though the point also often goes unnoticed.[18] Origen, though obviously valuing the text(s)

---

17 Let. Aris. 30.

18 See discussions in Edmon L. Gallagher, "The Septuagint's Fidelity to Its *Vorlage* in Greek Patristic Thought," in *XIV Congress of the International Organization for Septuagint and Cognate Studies, Helsinki, 2010*, ed. Melvin K. H. Peters, SCS 59

of the Greek Old Testament to a high degree, nevertheless devotes the first two columns of his Hexapla to the Hebrew, signaling its prime position. Other church fathers, in defending the use of the "Septuagint" text in circulation at the time (against, say, Aquila's recension), do so not because they think it should supplant the Hebrew—far from it. Rather, they value it because it is connected with the Hebrew and accurately reflects it. Even Augustine, though stridently endorsing the Greek Old Testament, nevertheless acknowledges the value of the Hebrew, especially since New Testament authors indeed use it at times in addition to the Greek.[19]

In short, the cumulative evidence suggests that normative Scripture has always been located not in the "Septuagint" but in the standard Hebrew text of the prophetic writers, passed on under the auspices of the priests and scribes of the Jerusalem temple. The fact that we lack a singular concrete copy of this standard temple text—yet have a variety of nonstandard texts—does not negate the evidence for its existence in antiquity and normativity today, as reconstructed.

Summary

We have outlined the evidence for why the Hebrew Bible, in terms of the threefold collection of books and the actual text of those books, should continue to be considered the normative authority for today's church. Where does that leave the "Septuagint"?

First, the Apocrypha, though not normative, should not be completely ignored by Protestants. Jerome's notion that it is useful for private devotional "edification" or learning is still insightful and should be

---

(Atlanta: SBL, 2013), 663–76; Gallagher, *Hebrew Scripture in Patristic Biblical Theory: Canon, Language, Text*, VCSup 114 (Leiden: Brill, 2012), 143–208.

19 Augustine, *Civ.* 18.43–44.

recovered; indeed, such a view was common in the Reformation but has faded over time.[20] Apocryphal books, though bearing no normative authority, can still be read with profit by Protestants.[21]

Second, the manuscripts of the Greek Old Testament are invaluable for editing the existing Masoretic Text to reconstruct the earliest, authentic form of the Hebrew. If the Greek Old Testament does, as far as we can judge, contain superior wording (recall examples in chap. 5), then it does exercise normative authority in such cases. But such authority points upstream to its Hebrew source text (which apparently was lost from the Masoretic tradition), not to itself.

Derivative Authority

A defense of the normative authority of the Hebrew canon and text does not end the discussion. Often scholars ask whether the New Testament authors' use of the Greek Old Testament is a "divine sanctioning of that form,"[22] such that, even if we adopt the Hebrew, we should adhere to the (so-called) "Septuagintal" text as being equally (if not more) authoritative.[23]

This debate results from an erroneous flattening of distinctions when it comes to the question of authority, which fails to give weight to the fact that the Greek Old Testament is a translation for those

---

20 Belgic Confession, art. 6; Book of Common Prayer, art. 6; *Synopsis Purioris Theologiae*, 3.37.

21 See Greg Lanier, "Can Protestants Be Edified by the Apocrypha?," The Gospel Coalition, June 20, 2019, https://www.thegospelcoalition.org/article/can-protestants-edified-apocrypha.

22 Edmon L. Gallagher, "The Septuagint in Patristic Sources," in *T&T Clark Handbook of Septuagint Research*, ed. William A. Ross and W. Edward Glenny (London: Bloomsbury T&T Clark, 2021), 255–67.

23 For a helpful taxonomy of approaches, see W. Edward Glenny, "The Septuagint and Biblical Theology," *Them* 41, no. 2 (2016): 263–78.

lacking direct access to the Hebrew words. We should thus approach the Greek as we would approach any other faithful translation of Scripture: it can possess derivative authority as the *word of God*, which stems from but is not the same thing as *Scripture*, as outlined in the prior section.[24] Let us unpack what we mean by derivative authority and then examine how it works in the New Testament.

What We Mean by Derivative Authority

As of 2020, portions of the Hebrew Bible and Greek New Testament have been translated into over 3,400 languages.[25] For centuries only a fraction of global Christians have read the Old Testament in Hebrew. Preachers around the world stand up to teach from Bibles in Bengali, Swahili, Mandarin, and a host of other languages that may not even have been around in the time of Paul or Moses. Yet they all rightly designate the Bible in their language as the "word of God." The underlying Hebrew of the Old Testament and Greek of the New Testament are deemed normative Scripture—the final judge of doctrinal issues. But in the day-to-day life of the church, the vernacular translation functions as God's word for memorization, teaching, evangelism, and worship.

The warrant for translation is embedded in the Bible itself and sharply contrasts with Islam, in which the only true Qur'an is Arabic. Multiplicity of languages dates at least as far back as Babel (Gen. 11) and is anticipated in God's dealings with Noah's sons (Gen. 9). The Abrahamic promise implies that language barriers must be crossed

---

24 On this distinction between translations as *word of God* and the original Hebrew/Greek as *Scripture*, see the Chicago Statement on Biblical Inerrancy (1978), art. 10, https://www.etsjets.org/files/documents/Chicago_Statement.pdf.

25 "2020 Scripture Access Statistics," Wycliffe Global Alliance, October 2020, accessed February 1, 2021, https://www.wycliffe.net/resources/statistics/.

in order for "all the families of the earth" to be blessed (Gen. 12:3). Hebrew- or Aramaic-speaking Jews were to reach people "of every tongue" (Zech. 8:23). Translation of the Torah likely began in the days of Ezra and Nehemiah (Neh. 8:8). Paul changed languages to accommodate his message to his hearer (Acts 21:40). The Aramaic sidenotes in the Gospels (e.g., Mark 5:41) likewise accommodate those who know only Greek, and the very fact that many of Jesus's speeches were in Aramaic but were translated into Greek implies that faithful translation is in some way authoritative.

Put differently, the mission to all peoples requires spreading the word of God in their languages, not forcing all into the same language (see Rev. 5:9). Though the early Christian movement debated the ongoing role of Torah and battled against Judaizers (e.g., Acts 15; Gal. 2–3), there was never a *linguistic* Judaizing movement. That is, no one in ancient Israel, Second Temple Judaism, or the early church argued that you must learn Hebrew in order to access the Law and the Prophets.

What does this mean? Simply put, for the Old Testament, the divine meaning and authorial purpose cannot reside strictly in the precise form of the Hebrew/Aramaic text per se but may be conveyed via accurate translation into any language. No translation is perfect, because no two languages are identical. But when sanctified by the Holy Spirit, a competent if imperfect translation of *Scripture*, which has normative authority, can and should be called the *word of God*, which has derived authority.[26] The former results from divine inspiration (in setting forth the words), the latter from providence (in accurately conveying meaning).

---

26 See further discussion in Karen H. Jobes, "'It Is Written': The Septuagint and Evangelical Doctrine of Scripture," in *Evangelical Scholarship, Retrospects and Prospects: Essays in Honor of Stanley N. Gundry*, ed. Dirk R. Buursma, Katya Covrett, and Verlyn D. Verbrugge (Grand Rapids, MI: Zondervan, 2017), 137–55.

This distinction is key to understanding the authority of each. For the Old Testament, the Hebrew remains normative. But "where a regard for the sense and truth was preserved," the Greek translation(s) held derivative authority for those who knew no Hebrew or who were addressing such an audience:[27] from early Greek-speaking Jews (Aristeas, Aristobulus, Demetrius, Eupolemus) to Philo and Josephus, New Testament authors, and many church fathers and early Christians. Without the Greek Old Testament, the word of God would have been greatly hindered.[28]

How Derivative Authority Works in the New Testament

Let us probe further the evidence for how derivative authority is expressed in the New Testament, reflecting on the apostolic authors' use of sources and quotation patterns.

BROADER USE OF SOURCES

As mentioned above, the mere fact that New Testament authors use the Greek Old Testament is often deemed an upgrade of its status. But we need to keep a broader picture in mind. Multiple times New Testament authors use a variant of an "it is written" formula when quoting a text that is not recognizably found in the Hebrew *or* Greek Old Testament. Sometimes they quote from a known source that is

27 Francis Turretin, *Institutes of Elenctic Theology*, trans. George Musgrave Giger, ed. James T. Dennison Jr. (Phillipsburg, NJ: P&R, 1992–1997), 1.14.7. The Westminster Confession of Faith (1.8) distinguishes between the "authentical" and "inspired" Scriptures in the original languages and the vernacular translations as the means by which the "Word of God dwell[s] in all." See also *Synopsis Purioris Theologiae*, 3.11.

28 Calvin aptly describes the "signal and miraculous work of God," whereby the spread of the Greek Old Testament helped keep knowledge of Israel's Scriptures alive after knowledge of Hebrew atrophied. *Institutes of the Christian Religion*, ed. John T. McNeill, trans. Ford Lewis Battles, LCC 20–21 (Louisville: Westminster John Knox, 1960), 1.8.10.

not canonical. And sometimes they directly draw on (but do not quote verbatim) information that is found only in Jewish tradition and not in the Old Testament. Consider the examples in table 7.2.

Table 7.2   New Testament Use of Nonbiblical Sources

"It is written" formula with unclear OT source*	Matt. 2:23 ("Nazarene")
	John 7:38 ("rivers of living water")
	1 Cor. 2:9 ("what no eye has seen")
	1 Cor. 9:10 ("the plowman . . . and the thresher")
	Eph. 5:14 ("awake, O sleeper")
	2 Tim. 2:19 (unknown "seal")
	James 4:5 ("he yearns jealously")
	2 Pet. 2:22 (wallowing pig proverb)
Quoting a non-biblical source	Acts 17:28–29 (Aratus and possibly Epimenedes)
	1 Cor. 15:33 (Menander)
	Titus 1:12 (Epimenedes)
	Jude 14–15 (1 Enoch 1.9)
Use of Jewish tradition	Acts 5:36; 21:38 (messianic uprisings also discussed by Josephus)
	2 Tim. 3:8 (Egyptian magicians Jannes and Jambres, not mentioned in Exodus)
	Heb. 11:35–37 (possibly Maccabean martyrdom stories)
	Jude 9 (Michael's battle with Satan over Moses's body)

*   For many of these passages, the cross-references of the critical editions of the Greek New Testament read simply, *unde* (Lat. "from where?").

Clearly, a New Testament author's use of a source, even one with an "it is written" formula, does not imbue it with inspired status or even imply that the author thought the source was inspired. Paul's use of the Greek poet Aratus and Jude's apparent use of 1 Enoch do not magically make those texts inspired or normative. That is, they do not become "Scripture" in the same sense as the Scripture in which they are quoted. Such inspired use of noninspired sources simply conveys that the information being used is *true* and thus pertinent to the argument being made. This distinction should also apply, at least as an initial starting point, to quotations of the Greek Old Testament. Let us go one step further.

QUOTATION PATTERNS

In the previous chapter, we set forth the data regarding New Testament quotation practices, but here we sketch a picture of the implications. As a recap, there are four patterns for specific quotations of the Old Testament in the New Testament (see table 7.3).

Table 7.3   Quotation Patterns in the New Testament

Pattern	Illustrative Example
Alignment with both the Hebrew and the Old Greek	Quotation of Lev. 19:18 in Matt. 19:19; Mark 12:31; Rom. 13:9
Alignment with the Hebrew but not the Old Greek	Quotation of Hos. 11:1 in Matt. 2:15, where the Hebrew "my son" is used instead of the Old Greek's "my children"
Alignment with the Old Greek but not the Hebrew	Quotation of Ps. 95[94]:7–11 in Heb. 3:7–11, where several words/phrases follow the Old Greek (e.g., "rebellion" and "testing") instead of the Hebrew ("Meribah" and "Massah")
Alignment with neither the Hebrew nor the Old Greek	Quotation of Isa. 10:22 in Rom. 9:27, which is meaningfully different from both the Hebrew and the Greek

The vast majority of quotations of the Old Testament in the New fall into the first pattern, which is unsurprising given the general quality of the Greek translations of the Old Testament (see chap. 3). A few dozen quotations fit into each of the other patterns, depending on the criteria one uses to parcel them out.[29] Such variability in the wording of quotations need not concern us, as if the New Testament authors were being sloppy; by ancient standards, the precision of their quotations is higher than often granted.[30]

Of additional significance is how the New Testament authors attribute these quotations. "It is written" or similar statements span all four patterns. In our small sampling above, we see the following: Romans 4:3 cites *graphē* (Gk. "writing"), Matthew 2:15 cites "what the Lord had spoken by the prophet," Hebrews 3:7 cites "the Holy Spirit," and Romans 9:27 cites the prophet Isaiah. And the attribution of the Psalm 69[68]:25 quotation in Acts 1:16–20—which aligns more closely with the Old Greek than with the Hebrew—covers all the bases: "the *graphē* . . . which the Holy Spirit spoke . . . by the mouth of David . . . in the Book of Psalms."

On top of this, it is important to note that different New Testament authors do not always perfectly match each other when quoting the *same* Old Testament passage in Greek. In addition to the examples in chapter 6 (quotations of the Decalogue and Isa. 6:9–10),

29 See Gleason Archer and Gregory Chirichigno, *Old Testament Quotations in the New Testament* (Chicago: Moody Press, 1983), xxv–xxxii.

30 Today's standards, driven by academic/journalistic rules on plagiarism, are much higher than in antiquity, when the main goal was not to give a word-for-word facsimile of a quoted source but to capture its essence. See Charles E. Hill, "'In These Very Words': Methods and Standards of Literary Borrowing in the Second Century," in *The Early Text of the New Testament*, ed. Charles E. Hill and Michael J. Kruger (Oxford: Oxford University Press, 2012), 261–81.

Table 7.4   Diverse Ways of Quoting the Same Old Testament Passage

OT Text	NT Quotation	Differences in How the OT Text Is Quoted
Gen. 2:24	Matt. 19:5; Mark 10:7; Eph. 5:31	Matthew omits the prefix on the verb "hold fast"; Ephesians uses a different initial conjunction and omits some of the articles ("the") in the Old Greek
Ex. 3:6	Matt. 22:32; Mark 12:26; Luke 20:37	Mark (in some manuscripts) and Luke omit the second and third articles in "the God of"
Deut. 25:4	1 Cor. 9:9; 1 Tim. 5:18	1 Corinthians uses a different verb for "muzzle"; 1 Timothy reverses the word order of the sentence
Ps. 110[109]:1	Matt 22:44; Mark 12:36; Luke 20:42–43; Acts 2:34–35; Heb. 1:13	Matthew and Mark use "under" instead of "footstool"
Zech. 9:9	Matt. 21:5; John 12:15	John uses "sitting" rather than "mounted," and he employs different terms for the "donkey's colt"

we could include those listed in table 7.4. Others could be added, but these samples suffice to show that the apostolic authors do not necessarily sanction a singular translation of a given Old Testament passage as exclusively "right."[31]

---

31 Some have argued that we know a Greek Old Testament translation is correct and thus fully normative when it is cited in the New Testament; these examples, however, show that such a rule of thumb is too simple, for in such cases where the apostolic authors do not always perfectly agree, how can we judge which translation is "correct"?

These lines of evidence come together to make a crucial point clear: the New Testament authors ascribe what we are calling derivative authority to multiple renderings of Scripture, including the Greek Old Testament, insofar as those renderings accurately express divine truth from God, the Spirit, the prophets, and the *graphē*. Sometimes (as covered in chap. 5), a given point made by a New Testament author relies specifically on the reading of the Greek Old Testament where it apparently deviates from the known Hebrew. Sometimes the same point could be made from any of the known textual forms, whether Hebrew or Greek. The authors did not see themselves as bound "to give as exact a representation of the original, in all its aspects and on every side, as possible; but only to give a true account of its teaching."[32] That is, the New Testament authors, in reaching a Greek world, prioritized the faithful communication of the *meaning* of an Old Testament source text higher than punctilious adherence to a set (Hebrew) *wording*.

Thus, when a New Testament author quotes wording from the Greek Old Testament as *graphē* or says, "as it is written," we can approach it much like we might a modern preacher who says, after reading from the NIV, "This is the word of the Lord." It does not necessarily convey that the Greek Old Testament is *Scripture* with normative authority[33] but rather the *word of God* with derivative authority in reaching a Greek-speaking audience. Its authority, in other words, is downstream from its normative source text. When the wording of the Greek Old Testament truly conveys the sense of Scripture, it is rightly quoted and applied as true by the New Testament authors.

---

32 Archibald Hodge and B. B. Warfield, "Inspiration," *Presbyterian Review* 6 (1881): 225–60.

33 Competent preachers may often indicate that they disagree with how the translation they are using renders something, showing that it is not perfect as a translation.

Summary

We have fleshed out how the Greek Old Testament bears derivative authority for the Greek-speaking church of its day: an authority that is not independent of but rather flows from its source. Let us state two takeaways.

First, quotations of the Greek Old Testament in the New Testament do not mean that the quoted textual form is itself inspired, nor that the textual form should necessarily replace the form of the Masoretic Text (if different), nor that the Greek Old Testament as a whole must be viewed as normative Scripture. Rather, it is only the specific truth claim made by the New Testament author himself, drawing on the wording of his Greek Old Testament text, that is itself inspired.[34] The apostolic writer does not impart inspiration into the quotation itself—as if transforming it into a little inspired morsel baked into an otherwise fallible slice of cake—nor to the "Septuagint" cake as a whole.[35] As shown above, they do not even always use identical wording of the same Old Testament passage. Thus, the New Testament authors' use of the Greek Old Testament does not sanction it as Scripture for us today, since it was not singular Scripture (as defined above) for them. It was, by God's providence, a vehicle of truth for evangelizing a Hellenized world,

---

34 Turretin writes, "The quotations in the New Testament from the Septuagint are not authentic *per se* . . . but *per accidens* inasmuch as they were drawn into the sacred context by the evangelists." *Institutes*, 14.8.

35 Jobes summarizes it well (and with a different metaphor): "Does this mean the OT verses quoted in the NT are little inspired nuggets embedded in the otherwise uninspired Septuagint text, like diamonds in rock? Not at all. Divine inspiration applies only to the semantic contribution specifically made by the Septuagint quotations by virtue of becoming part of the inspired New Testament text as used in their specific New Testament context." "'It Is Written,'" 154.

bearing an authority derived from the Hebrew Scripture insofar as it accurately reflects it.[36]

Second, the Septuagint as a whole can be used in the same way as, say, a modern translation of the Old Testament. As discussed in chapter 3, approaches used to translate the Greek Old Testament vary, just as they do for modern translations. Some books are more closely tied to the Hebrew source (such as Numbers), while others are less so (such as Job); that is, some are like the NASB but others like the NLT. Across the spectrum, the Greek Old Testament—not just the small portions quoted in the New Testament—can be read, even quoted, as long as its limits and fallibility are kept in mind.[37] This leads to one more form of authority.

Interpretive Authority

A final way to look at the Greek Old Testament is as a "resource for doing Christian theology."[38] Given the important ways in which it reflects early Jewish interpretation of Scripture and shaped New Testament and patristic exegesis, we would argue that the Greek Old Testament should be seen as bearing a kind of interpretive authority.

Let us be clear what we mean. The Reformation instinct is that "Scripture interprets Scripture"; the normative authority norms itself. But this principle does not impose strict biblicism ("me and my

36 As Robert Cara pointed out to us, this pattern of Old Testament citation in the New Testament fits within the "good and necessary consequences" of the "true and full sense" of Scripture, per Westminster Confession of Faith 1.6 and 1.9.

37 Turretin states, "No more authority is to be ascribed to this version than to those made by human industry." *Institutes*, 14.6, citing Joannes Morinus.

38 J. Ross Wagner, "The Septuagint and the 'Search for the Christian Bible,'" in *Scripture's Doctrine and Theology's Bible: How the New Testament Shapes Christian Dogmatics*, ed. Markus Bockmuehl and Alan J. Torrance (Grand Rapids, MI: Baker Academic, 2008), 17–28.

Bible alone") or rule out insight from the broader church tradition.[39] As shown above, even the New Testament authors were not strict biblicists, in that they engaged with Jewish and Hellenistic traditions too. Thus, it can be helpful to consider the Greek translations as a *commentary* on the Hebrew Scriptures—part of the chorus of voices that should be engaged in studying the Bible. They are certainly not infallible, and treating the Greek Old Testament *only* as commentary can be too restrictive (as implied by the prior sections). Yet the Greek Old Testament should still be given more attention in this capacity than it currently receives among many (especially Protestant) Christians.

Such an approach to the Greek Old Testament would, in fact, be a retrieval of the practice of the ancient church. It is often forgotten that the vast majority of early debates that hashed out orthodox doctrine took place in the Greek-speaking East. From Justin Martyr's arguments with Jewish interlocutors to the ecumenical councils on the Trinity and Christology helmed by such figures as Athanasius, the discussions were typically conducted in Greek. And their Old Testament text was almost exclusively what they called the "Seventy," though with occasional reference to Aquila and the other recensions. The Old Greek translation of Isaiah 7:14 (*parthenos*) was essential to incarnation discussions. The notion of the "creation" or "preexistence" of "wisdom" (*sophia*) in the Greek of Proverbs 8 played a role in debates on Arianism. The different Greek forms of the Danielic "son of man" passage played a role in many church fathers' articulation of Christ's human nature. While the Greek Old Testament does not have a theology that

39 See Michael Allen and Scott R. Swain, *Reformed Catholicity: The Promise of Retrieval for Theology and Biblical Interpretation* (Grand Rapids, MI: Baker Academic, 2015).

differs in significant ways from the Hebrew Bible,[40] the following is generally true:

> The formative theological debates of the second through fifth centuries were conducted in constant dialogue with the Septuagint, so much so that the triumphant orthodoxy formulated its doctrines in reliance on the language of this particular version.[41]

Commentaries are sometimes wrong. But that does not mean they should be ignored wholesale. From this vantage point, the Greek Old Testament can and should be considered as having a prime, though fallible, place in understanding the history of interpreting the Hebrew Scriptures.[42]

This angle on authority applies not only to the Greek Old Testament as a whole but also to the well-known cases surveyed in chapter 5, where the shape of a book or passage in the Greek tradition differs meaningfully from the traditional Hebrew text (e.g., shorter versions of the David and Goliath narrative, Jeremiah, and Ezekiel). With rare exception, these variant Greek forms offer little text-critical help in reconstructing the normative Hebrew Scripture. Moreover, because they differ so substantially from the known Hebrew, they cannot be considered mere translations, and thus they lack derivative author-

---

40 As noted by Karen H. Jobes, "The Septuagint as Scripture in the Early Church," in *The Sacred Text: Excavating the Texts, Exploring the Interpretations, and Engaging the Theologies of the Christian Scriptures*, ed. Michael Bird and Michael Pahl (Piscataway, NJ: Gorgias, 2010), 24.

41 Gallagher, "Septuagint," 265.

42 Wagner describes the Septuagint as forming a part of the "complete canon" or "broader canon" of biblical truth in Christianity. "Septuagint," 24. We would quibble with the use of "canon" here, but the main point is illuminating.

ity. Rather, they are best seen as part of a broader Jewish spectrum of "resignifying" the biblical books—paraphrasing or recasting them in new ways.[43] As such, they are helpful windows into early Jewish interpretation.[44]

All this leads to a final takeaway: *in studying the theology of the New Testament as it engages with the Old Testament, the Greek Old Testament* must *play a key interpretive role, not just the Masoretic Hebrew.* The Greek Old Testament helps us breathe the air the New Testament authors were breathing in their day. It sometimes contains a superior reading for the Old Testament text. It sheds invaluable light on how certain words, phrases, and ideas circulated in a Judeo-Christian context. And most important, it is often used by the New Testament authors instead of the Hebrew. Therefore, any attempt to study a New Testament quotation of an Old Testament passage and its surrounding context is impoverished if the Greek Old Testament is not consulted. It is a key link that translates and interprets the Old and thus cannot be bracketed out when analyzing and interpreting the New.[45]

Concluding Thoughts

Taking stock of where we have been, it is clear that the question posed about the authority of the "Septuagint" is more complex than a yes

---

43 This spectrum of "resignification" includes the so-called "rewritten Bible" genre (e.g., Jubilees, Liber antiquitatum biblicarum, Genesis Apocryphon) as well as Aramaic Targums.

44 The same could be said for the longer additions in the Greek New Testament; even if one denies that, say, the story of the adulterous woman (John 7:53–8:11) or the long ending of Mark (16:9–20) are "Scripture," they still gives insight into the early church's interpretation of the story of Jesus.

45 See further in Glenny, "Septuagint."

or no. As a bridge from the Old Testament to the New Testament, its authority takes three forms, as shown in table 7.5.

Table 7.5   Expanded Framework for "Authority"

	Normative	Derivative	Interpretive
Key concept	Scripture	Word of God	Commentary
Description	Inspired canon and text used for faith and practice	Providentially guided translations of Scripture that can convey God's word to God's people	Illuminating insights that can assist God's people in understanding Scripture
Role of the Greek OT	Hebrew is normative canon and text; Greek OT often plays a key text-critical role in reconstructing the text	Greek OT was the word of God for the early Greek-speaking church; NT quotations do not sanction it as Scripture as a whole but show the quoted text to be true	Apostolic and patristic use of the Greek OT dignify its role as a (fallible) source for theology

So should *you* use the Greek Old Testament? Our answer, of course, is yes. But our equally important point is that it depends on what you are using it for, since what kind of authority one ascribes to it shapes how one uses it.

You should not follow the broader canon found in certain Greek manuscripts—but you should read the Apocrypha to understand the Jewish and early Christian world.

You should not preach from the "Septuagint" as if it were a unified, singular entity that can serve equally well as "inspired" Scripture for today's church—but you should consult it text-critically as a key source for reconstructing the Hebrew text.

You should not give the Greek Old Testament the final say in matters of theological debate—but you should recognize its importance in shaping the biblical theology of the New Testament authors and early church.

You should not ignore the Greek Old Testament as an irrelevant obscurity in your Bible's footnotes—but you should give it full attention when seeking to understand the Old Testament, the New Testament, the use of the former in the latter, and church history.

Appendix

Ten Key Questions about
the Septuagint

WE HAVE COVERED A LOT of complex terrain in this introduction to the "Septuagint." The following list provides common questions that ministers and Bible teachers may get, along with brief responses.

1. What Is the "Septuagint"?

The "Septuagint" (often abbreviated LXX) is a catchall term that usually refers to the corpus of ancient Greek translations of the Hebrew Bible. It can be used in various senses depending on context: the initial effort and result of translating the Pentateuch (Genesis–Deuteronomy); the translations of all the books of the Hebrew Bible, including some later revisions; or the collection of Greek writings that include translations of the Hebrew books as well as additional writings known as the Apocrypha.

2. Where Can I Find the "Septuagint"?

Modern translations. There are two recent English translations, each with slightly different philosophies.[1]

Penner, Ken M., and Rick Brannan, eds. *The Lexham English Septuagint.*
Bellingham, WA: Lexham, 2019. (LES)
Pietersma, Albert, and Benjamin G. Wright, eds. *A New English Transla-
tion of the Septuagint.* Oxford: Oxford University Press, 2008. (NETS)

Greek semicritical editions. Texts of semicritical editions include the full, standard corpus but were produced using a limited manuscript base.[2]

Rahlfs, Alfred, and Robert Hanhart, eds. *Septuaginta: Editio Altera.*
Stuttgart: Deutsche Bibelgesellschaft, 2006.
Swete, Henry Barclay, ed. *The Old Testament in Greek, according to the
Septuagint.* Cambridge: Cambridge University Press, 1896.

Greek editions. The most exhaustive scholarly text is known as the Göttingen edition, which aims to reconstruct the Old Greek text itself. Not all books in the corpus are yet complete, but texts are still in production.[3]

1   On these philosophies and those involved in other translations, see William A. Ross, "The Septuagint and Modern Language Translations," in *T&T Clark Handbook of Septuagint Research*, ed. William A. Ross and W. Edward Glenny (London: Bloomsbury T&T Clark, 2021), 329–44.
2   Note that the older editions are available freely online. The edition by Rahlfs and Hanhart is also accessible at the Deutsche Bibelgesellschaft website, www.academic-bible.com/en/online-bibles.
3   Bibliographic details for each volume can be found at the Göttingen Academy of Sciences and Humanities website, http://adw-goe.de/en/research/completed-research

Wevers, John W., Robert Hanhart, Alfred Rahlfs, Joseph Ziegler, Werner Kappler, Felix Albrecht, Peter J. Gentry, et al., eds. *Septuaginta Vetus Testamentum Graecum*. Auctoritate Academiae Scientiarum Gottingensis editum. Göttingen: Vandenhoeck & Ruprecht, 1939–.

An older project known as the "larger Cambridge edition" also aimed to produce a critical text, but it was based on less textual evidence than the Göttingen edition. This project is incomplete and is no longer underway, but it still remains useful.

Brooke, Alan E., Norman McLean, and Henry St. J. Thackeray, eds. *The Old Testament in Greek*. Cambridge: Cambridge University Press, 1906–1940.

Editions of recensions. The following texts attempt to reconstruct various recensions as discussed in chapter 4. Note that Field's edition of the Hexapla is not a running text but provides only word- or phrase-level readings, owing to the scant evidence available.[4]

Fernández Marcos, Natalio, and José Ramón Busto Saiz, eds. *El Texto Antioqueno de la Biblia Griega*. Madrid: Instituto de Filología CSIC, 1989–1996.
Field, Frederick. *Origenis Hexaplorum Quae Supersunt, sive Veterum Interpretum Graecorum in Totum Vetus Testamentum Fragmenta*. Oxford: Clarendon, 1867–1875.

-projects/akademienprogramm/septuaginta-unternehmen/publications/septuaginta
-vetus-testamentum-graecum, accessed June 22, 2021.

4 Field's important edition is being updated by scholars involved in the Hexapla Institute. The completed installments in that project can be found on their website, https://hexapla.org, accessed June 22, 2021.

3. When, Where, Why, and How Was the Greek Old Testament Produced?

Translation began with the Pentateuch in or near Alexandria, Egypt, in the mid-third century BC. Other books were translated in the subsequent centuries in Egypt and possibly Palestine. The translators were multilingual Jews who may have been motivated by external factors (a sociopolitical need to have the Jewish law accessible in Greek, given Ptolemaic rule) and internal factors (a religious need to make Scripture available to Greek-speaking Jews who did not read Hebrew). Viewed as a corpus, the translation is not uniform, but the books manifest numerous approaches and layers. Most translators represented each word of their source text with Greek, in order, as their default approach. Other translators were less concerned with that goal and felt free to be creative in how they rendered their text (or worked from a source text that differed from the standard Masoretic Text used today). Still others took a more exacting and sequential approach to representing each linguistic element in their source text as they translated. In all cases, the translators demonstrate in sometimes surprising or subtle ways their artistic competence and facility with Greek.

4. How Did the Greek Old Testament Get to Us Today?

The Greek Old Testament was transmitted over the centuries through the process of hand copying by Jewish and Christian scribes. This inevitably produced both unintentional and intentional textual variants, which scholars try to sort out in order to approximate the earliest wording. In addition, there were efforts over time to revise the translations, often to bring them closer to the Hebrew text, among other linguistic goals. Other full retranslations also occurred, including those by Aquila, Symmachus, and Theodotion; Origen's Hexaplaric recension; and the so-called Antiochene (or Lucianic) recension.

5. How Does the Greek Old Testament Help Us Study the Canon and Text of the Old Testament?

In terms of canon, the Apocrypha—for example, 1–2 Maccabees, Judith, Tobit—are considered "deuterocanonical" by the Roman Catholic and Orthodox Churches largely because of their association with the growing collection of Greek translations of canonical books. Most Jews, however, did not acknowledge them as scriptural and instead pointed to the normativity of the Hebrew books—a perspective ultimately adopted by the Protestant church during the Reformation. In terms of textual criticism, the Greek Old Testament is valuable for helping restore the authentic text of the Hebrew Bible. While the best complete Hebrew manuscript is from the Middle Ages, the Greek Old Testament provides evidence that is up to a millennium earlier to help make corrections where erroneous readings have entered the Hebrew tradition.

6. How Does the Greek Old Testament Give Us a Window into the Ancient Jewish World?

Every translation is by definition a kind of commentary. So the Greek Old Testament gives us a glimpse into how ancient Jews interpreted Scripture, not only when they adhere closely to the Hebrew but especially when they revise it in such a way that gives telltale insights into their use of language or views of contemporary events, social context, and even theology.

7. Did the New Testament Authors Use the Greek Old Testament?

Yes, but in a qualified sense. Given that virtually the entire Roman world of the first century AD spoke Greek, it is natural that the apostolic authors wrote the New Testament in Greek. As they did so, in many cases New Testament authors quoted from the Old Testament using a Greek text that would have been familiar to their audience (at Rome, Corinth, Ephesus, etc.). New Testament authors did not have a tidy, leather-bound copy of the "Septuagint" that they could pull off the shelf—books did not yet exist as such in the ancient world. Nevertheless, it is true that these Old Testament quotations often (but not always) adhere closely to the wording of the Old Greek, even when it deviates from the Masoretic Hebrew text that we know today.

8. Does the Greek Old Testament Have Any Authority in Today's Church?

Based on the historical arguments presented in this book, the Hebrew Bible should be preferred as the normative canon and text, although the Greek Old Testament plays a helpful role in establishing the latter. The Greek Old Testament is valuable *as a translation* of the Hebrew text and was rightly used by the apostolic circle and early church as the "word of God" in that derivative sense (much like modern translations). Finally, the Greek Old Testament as an ancient "commentary" offers helpful but fallible insight for the task of interpreting the Hebrew Bible.

9. How Should I Handle Seemingly Threatening Issues That Arise When the "Septuagint" Comes Up in Ministry Settings?

For many evangelicals, the "Septuagint" can come across as threatening for various reasons, though each has a good response:

- Its history and character are complex, sometimes to the point of seeming esoteric. We suggest that getting more familiar with the basics of the topic through books like this one will help.

- It raises uncomfortable questions about the inerrancy of the Old Testament because it provides data showing that the transmission of the Hebrew text was not pristine. We would remind readers that the existence of textual variants or even divergent versions of specific books (such as Jeremiah) does not mean that there was no stable and normative text, for which there is solid evidence.

- The association of the Greek Old Testament with the Apocrypha often taints the former as dangerous or even fraudulent, particularly among some in KJV-only circles. We should, however, approach the Apocrypha as made up of helpful but nonscriptural writings, similar to the church fathers. The Apocrypha's much later bundling as part of the "Septuagint" is neither something we need to adopt today nor something that makes the Greek Old Testament bankrupt in itself.

- The New Testament use of the Greek Old Testament, particularly where it differs from the Hebrew, may raise questions about the inerrancy of the New Testament. For this we remind readers that the New Testament authors are not sanctioning the Greek wording (as a whole) nor showing the Hebrew to be wrong (per se) but simply adopting a form of the Old Testament text that is true and valid for their argument.

10. If I Want to Learn More, Where Should I Turn?

To explore the topics of this book further, we recommend the following resources, listed in alphabetical order:

Aitken, James K., ed. *T&T Clark Companion to the Septuagint*. London: T&T Clark, 2015.

Dines, Jennifer M. *The Septuagint*. Understanding the Bible and Its World. London: T&T Clark, 2004.

Fernández Marcos, Natalio. *The Septuagint in Context: Introduction to the Greek Version of the Bible.* Translated by Wilfred G. E. Watson. 2nd ed. Leiden: Brill, 2000.

Fernández Marcos, Natalio, and María Victoria Spottorno Díaz-Caro, eds. *La Biblia Griega Septuaginta.* Salamanca: Ediciones Sígueme, 2008–2013.

Harl, Marguerite, et al., eds. *La Bible d'Alexandrie LXX.* Paris: Cerf, 1986–.

Jellicoe, Sidney. *The Septuagint and Modern Study.* Oxford: Clarendon, 1968.

Jobes, Karen H., and Moisés Silva. *Invitation to the Septuagint.* 2nd ed. Grand Rapids, MI: Baker Academic, 2015.

Kraus, Wolfgang, and Martin Karrer, eds. *Septuaginta Deutsch: Das Griechische Alte Testament in Deutscher Übersetzung.* Stuttgart: Deutsche Bibelgesellschaft, 2009. (LXX.D)

Kreuzer, Siegfried, ed. *Introduction to the LXX.* Translated by David A. Brenner and Peter Altmann. Waco, TX: Baylor University Press, 2019.

Lanier, Gregory R., and William A. Ross, eds. *Septuaginta: A Reader's Edition.* 2 vols. Peabody, MA: Hendrickson, 2018.

Ross, William A., and W. Edward Glenny, eds. *T&T Clark Handbook of Septuagint Research.* London: Bloomsbury T&T Clark, 2021.

Salvesen, Alison G., and Timothy Michael Law, eds. *The Oxford Handbook of the Septuagint.* Oxford: Oxford University Press, 2021.

Swete, Henry Barclay. *An Introduction to the Old Testament in Greek.* Cambridge: Cambridge University Press, 1914.

General Index

Scripture Index

Also Available from Greg Lanier

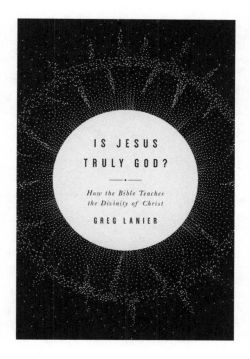

Is Jesus Truly God? invites readers to explore
the humanity and divinity of Jesus Christ by looking
at six key truths presented in the Scriptures
and later developed in the ecumenical creeds.

For more information, visit **crossway.org**.